V CUISINE
The Art of New Vegan Cooking

V CUISINE
The Art of New Vegan Cooking

Angeline Linardis

whitecap

For more information, contact Whitecap Books, 351 Lynn Avenue, North Vancouver, British Columbia, Canada V7J 2C4. Visit our website at www.whitecap.ca.

Edited by Judy Y. Smith
Proofread by Susan Falk
Design by Michelle Mayne
Typeset by Grace Partridge and Chrissy Davey
Food Photography by Tracey Kusiewicz
Kitchenware generously provided by Cookworks
1548 West Broadway, Vancouver, B.C., Canada V6J 5K9 604-731-1148
377 Howe Street, Vancouver, B.C., Canada V6C 3N2 604-662-4918
www.cookworks.ca

Printed in Canada by Friesens

Library and Archives Canada Cataloguing in Publication
Linardis, Angeline, 1962-
V cuisine: the art of new vegan cooking / Angeline Linardis.
Includes index.
ISBN 978-1-55285-903-2
ISBN 1-55285-903-7
1. Vegan cookery. I. Title.
TX837.L55 2007   641.5´636   C2007-901698-7

The publisher acknowledges the financial support of the Government of Canada through the Book Publishing Industry Development Program (BPIDP) and the province of British Columbia through the Book Publishing Tax Credit.

This book is dedicated to my family who inspired me to create V Cuisine in the first place and to all the amazing supporters of V Cuisine over the years. And to all great explorers of food delights who aren't afraid to try something different. Cheers!

TABLE OF CONTENTS

Do you like to be jazzed? Are you a bit of a rebel? V Cuisine is for vegans, vegetarians and anyone seeking fresh flavors, colors, textures and fun. Never boring, rarely fattening and packing a big nutritional boost, V Cuisine is the evolution of the best of vegan food and cooking.

V Cuisine is bold and exciting—it's all about creativity. It includes decadent dinners, velvety soups and sensual sauces. It's about fruity sweets laced with tiny traces of vanilla and cinnamon and other tongue-teasing extracts. If food is sex, then V Cuisine is the ultimate orgy.

V Cuisine means no dieting, no counting calories and no starving. It's all about giving your body what it needs. There's no bland food here—it's about vitality and taste.

Whole grains, beans, vegetables and fruits (and as little processed food as possible) star in this cuisine. Since there's no deep-frying at all, no butters or margarines, and only olive oil used moderately, the fat content is low.

V Cuisine is fantastic for kids because the meals and snacks are colorful and portable. Finger foods in various shapes served with tasty dips and spreads captivate kids. Most of these foods are easy to prepare so that parents can easily incorporate them into their day.

V Cuisine is spicy. Discovering new flavors is the name of the game. Your kitchen is an experimental lab. Sage isn't just for stuffing and hot sauce goes way beyond Mexican fare. Try curries, cumin and organic dill. Dive into fragrant basil, chervil and mints. It's about infused olive oils, peppery sauces and bright hits of lemon. Nutmegs, citrusy-sweet orange rinds and woody cinnamon sticks will rev up your senses. And garlic! Roasted, toasted, pickled and raw, garlic always gives a boost and a jolt.

The image of the long-haired, sandal-wearing, granola-crunching, tie-dyed hippy of the '60s is blasted away with V Cuisine. It's cool and people are interested in a big way. Some want to embrace the lifestyle; others just want to taste what looks good. It offers something for everyone—V Cuisine is the surprise hit of every gathering.

And V Cuisine is friends and family-oriented. Just because there's no turkey at Thanksgiving, doesn't mean there's no gathering! V Cuisine includes rich sauces, seasonal vegetables, fluffy stuffings, heavenly salads and scrumptious desserts. It's about creating new traditions that don't pop the zipper on your pants or put you to sleep for 12 hours afterward. V Cuisine is about spending time with people, not stressing over what to eat.

I'm Angeline. I hope that by the end of this book you'll feel like you know me. I want to be like your friend, your big sister, your mom—but without the judgment, only the fun. Whatever your age, whatever your situation, I want to jazz you about eating well. So, if I can help you create recipes you love, I'm all over that.

In the early '90s, when I was 29 years old, I was fat. I'll never know my exact weight because I had long since quit weighing myself. Put it this way: I'm 5'2" and I would guess I weighed at least 200 pounds. I didn't have an eating disorder. I was, however, a social eater who had plenty of occasions to attend. I never perceived myself as a fat person but I knew it wasn't really the way I was meant to be.

I was too dumpy to exercise and could barely breathe when I tried. Even if I went for a short walk, I'd end up gasping on the ground. Every time I went to doctors, they said I was asthmatic and tried to put me on inhalers. I always said no.

I was popping antacids like a maniac, but still always had what they would now call acid reflux disease. Then I developed hormone problems. My body wasn't producing enough progesterone. Although this is common in women in the menopausal zone, I wasn't prepared for it at 29. The symptoms were ugly; I felt disgusting in general and drastic measures were in order.

I gave up dairy and within the first week, I was no longer popping antacids and my lungs felt better. I also lost several pounds. Then I decided to give up red meat and pork. I never cared much for them anyway, so it was no big sacrifice for me, to be honest.

Within a couple of months, I knew I was onto something big. I'd lost about 30 pounds and loved everything I was eating. I had discovered a whole new world of food. Every day I was excited about another new ingredient or recipe. Suddenly I was eating a lot of things that as a kid I heard were "bad" or fattening, like potatoes. My lungs were absolutely clear and I had energy to burn. It was exhilarating. I felt light.

I had cut down on eating fish and chicken to a couple of times a month. Even though I still liked them, I found that after eating them I felt heavy, less energetic and as if something unclean was in my body. I'm not suggesting that anyone else should feel this way—it's just me. So I cut it out. The big deal was not only the health improvement, but also the energy boost. I wasn't dragging myself around any more.

After cutting out a final few products, I was basically vegan. The only exceptions were honey and Worcestershire sauce (which contains anchovies). I had lost all the excess weight and was fit and healthy. The hormone problems went away and I went on to have three more kids (I'd had a boy before all this started, then three little girls later on).

I've raised my three daughters on a vegan diet and my husband became vegan too eventually, which was a shock because he loved meat. He loved all the stuff I was making, and even said things like: "Wow, you can really taste all the other things on the pizza when it's not covered with cheese." Trust me, I practically fainted when he said that.

I never would have continued if I'd found it boring, or if the vegetarian ingredients just didn't cut it. I had taught cooking classes before, but began specializing exclusively in vegan classes using all the new ingredients I'd discovered.

That's how I've come to write this book. I love creating new recipes around this lifestyle every day and I want to give it to you with a fresh, fun attitude.

The Honey Thing

Normally, vegans don't eat honey. I do feed it to my family on occasion. It has been said that honey products have health benefits related to the ingredients in royal jelly, bee pollen and the honey itself.

If you don't want anything to do with honey, just ignore any reference I've made to it. It's the only non-vegan ingredient you'll find in the book. You can easily replace it with any other sugar. I've used agave syrup, brown rice syrup and barley malt syrup (available in natural food stores) as alternatives to the honey in these recipes. These are vegan products that have distinct flavors and work perfectly. They're also similar in consistency to honey. So use what works for you.

There's a soup for every mood. A good soup can warm you up on a cold day or refresh you on a summer evening. Soups can be light, brothy, rich 'n creamy or heavy-duty. Soup is a one-pot wonder and a great meal year-round.

Even if you have just two or three good soups in your repertoire, they'll serve you well over time. Simply increase your meal-making potential by developing some variations.

Imagine all the colorful components you can toss into soups, like bright, chopped herbs and bits of vibrant vegetables. If you're in the mood for noodles, add some. If you love artichokes or roasted red peppers, toss a few in. Maybe you want to include whole grains in your diet, but aren't ready to eat a large quantity of, say, spelt. Throw some in a soup to add texture and great taste.

If you find something a bit bland, but don't want to add salt, give the soup a good squirt of fresh lemon. Or better yet, lime. Try a drizzle of hot sauce or Indonesian soy. Use zested orange rind to add that extra bit of zing. If you want to add richness, try a little toasted sesame oil.

Why not make a gremolata to top off your soup? Traditionally, a gremolata is minced parsley, grated lemon rind and garlic, but toasted, chopped nuts, tiny bits of green onion, sesame seeds and freshly chopped herbs all work well. Presentation and color are super important, and all of these ideas add taste too.

In V Cuisine, there are no rules. These recipes are suggestions to rev you up. The possibilities for wildly good soups are endless, so create your own custom soup today.

Tomato Tornado

SERVES 4–6

A steamy, creamy bowl of tomato soup can warm up your insides on a damp, cold day. Make ahead, serve with salad and crusty bread. This is heavenly topped with a combo of crushed pumpkin seeds and toasted pecans, with a sprinkle of nutritional yeast. As with all things tomato, if you have any fresh basil, throw it in for the perfect finishing touch.

2 medium onions, chopped
2 or more stalks celery, chopped
4 cloves garlic, chopped
1 Tbsp (15 mL) olive oil
any ripe tomatoes you have kicking around, chopped
2 cups (500 mL) plum tomatoes (fresh or canned), or
    tomato sauce
2 cups (500 mL) unsweetened soy milk (or more as desired)
1 tsp (5 mL) dried basil
salt and pepper to taste

Put the onions, celery and garlic into a pot and cook on medium to high heat in the olive oil. Stir constantly until the onions are translucent. Add the tomatoes (fresh or canned) and then add enough water to cover the vegetables and turn the heat down to medium. Cover the pot and simmer well for at least 20 minutes, or until all vegetables are tender. Blend with an upright or hand blender until smooth and creamy. Add soy milk and season to taste.

You can heat and serve it immediately but I prefer to add a little extra soy milk or water and simmer it over low heat for another 20 minutes to an hour. Before simmering, add any extra seasonings you wish and then the flavors can really meld.

I'm not a big tomato chunk fan, so I like this soup perfectly puréed. But for those of you who are, you can leave some unblended.

Having your fancy friends over, dahhling? Cook the soup down until lovely and thick and then add 1 cup (250 mL) of good red wine, ½ cup (125 mL) of finely chopped, softened sun-dried tomatoes and some chopped fresh tarragon. Divinely impressive!

Feeling Greek? Add 1 tsp (5 mL) of cinnamon and 2 tsp (10 mL) of oregano to the tomato soup. It's a nice change from the ordinary. Or just cook it with a cinnamon stick in it, to be removed before eating.

For a wicked sauce that's great on almost anything, simmer 1 cup (250 mL) of the soup with the same amount of dry sherry. Add ½ cup (125 mL) of shallots and stir until it gets nice and thick.

Cream of Broccoli Dream

SERVES 4

For this rich and delicious soup, use as much broccoli as you can. If it's in season and you can afford to fill a whole pot, great. If not, I'd say 2 cups (500 mL) of broccoli is fine; it'll just have more of a supporting role.

2 medium onions, chopped
3 cloves garlic, chopped
2 Tbsp (30 mL) olive oil
2 Tbsp (30 mL) flour (optional, for thickness)
2 cups (500 mL) broccoli (or more), chopped
1 potato, chopped (optional)
2 cups (500 mL) unsweetened soy milk
salt and pepper to taste
freshly grated nutmeg (optional)

Sauté the onions and garlic in olive oil in a hot pot until the onions are translucent. For a thicker version, add the flour, whisking constantly, to make a roux. Then add a little liquid (water or soy milk) as you stir it, so it doesn't burn. You just want to cook the flour a little. Add a bit more liquid and stir till smooth. Then add the broccoli. Add the potato, if desired. Then add the soy milk, and if that doesn't cover the vegetables, add some water until they're covered. Put a lid on the pot and cook on medium heat until everything's tender.

Blend completely with an upright or hand blender if you want a smooth and creamy result. Or reserve a portion of the cooked broccoli, blend the rest until smooth and then add the reserved part back in. This makes for a more textural soup.

Add salt and pepper, and nutmeg, if you desire. If you don't have the nutmeg, you could add a pinch of ground cumin if you like that.

This soup is fantastic with a raw vegetable salad topped with a light vinaigrette dressing. Toasted nuts or polenta croutons tossed on top will make it even dreamier.

Albert Broccoli produced the kids' classic movie *Chitty Chitty Bang Bang*. It was his family that crossbred plants to create the plant we know as broccoli.

There's purple broccoli! Although the taste is the same as the regular variety, and most of it is green, the florets have a gorgeous purple cast to them. This would be terrific in a cold salad, so that purple color stays intact, or cook lightly.

If you have someone in your house who's not crazy about the stalk, try peeling it with a peeler. It will be more tender this way and perhaps more desirable to The Picky Eater!

Out of This World Roasted Cauliflower Soup

SERVES 6 OR MORE

If you're into comfort food, this is your recipe. Even though there's an extra step to roast the vegetables here, I think you'll find the extra effort worth it. The rich flavor of roasting infuses this soup. It has a sophisticated flavor, even though the ingredients are quite ordinary.

2 Tbsp (30 mL) olive oil
6 cloves garlic, chopped
2 medium onions, chopped
1 red pepper, chopped
1 tomato, chopped
1 small zucchini, chopped
1 full head of cauliflower, chopped
pinch of basil and oregano
pinch of nutmeg
3 cups unsweetened soy milk (or veg broth)
salt and pepper to taste

Preheat oven to 425°F (220°C). Put all the ingredients, except for the soy milk, salt and pepper into a small roasting or lasagna pan. Toss them well. Bake them covered with foil for about 25 minutes. Remove the foil and bake for another 25 minutes, giving a stir occasionally so that the vegtables don't stick too much. You want them to turn golden brown, but not burn, so add a little liquid or turn down the heat if necessary.

The next step is to blend up the soup. I do this in a pot with a hand blender. Just add the roasted vegetables to the soy milk in a pot. If the soy milk doesn't come up to the top of the vegetables, add a bit of water. Then blend it to almost smooth. Or just add it to your upright blender, if you prefer. You can blend it thoroughly or only slightly, depending on what you like. Then transfer it to the pot.

You really only have to heat this soup up till it's hot for it to be ready to eat. I like to simmer it on low, covered for about an hour though. If you want it thicker, you can simmer it uncovered until it reaches the desired consistency. Season it with salt and pepper, and serve.

You can add lemon juice to the cooking water when boiling cauliflower to keep it white.

Mark Twain, the great American humorist who wrote *Tom Sawyer*, *Huckleberry Finn* and a ton of other delightful stuff said, "Cauliflower is nothing but a cabbage with a college education." It is a member of the cabbage family.

In the '70s an orange variety of cauliflower was discovered in Canada, growing wild. Agricultural experts at Cornell University developed a hybrid and now it's becoming available in grocery stores.

Who knew? A head of cauliflower is actually called a curd. There you go—a good dairy replacement!

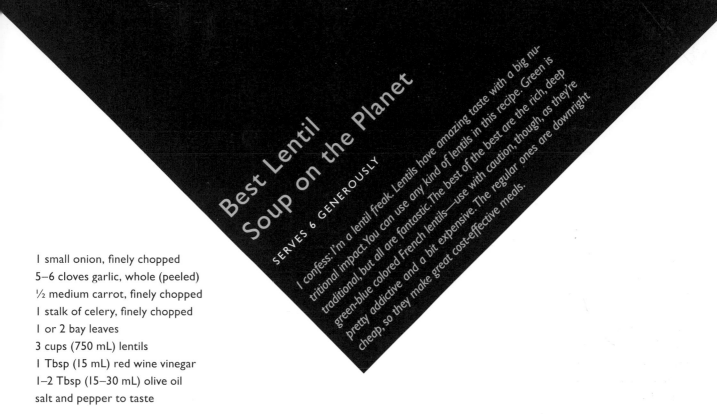

Best Lentil Soup on the Planet

SERVES 6 GENEROUSLY

I confess: I'm a lentil freak. Lentils have amazing taste with a big nutritional impact. You can use any kind of lentils in this recipe. Green is traditional, but all are fantastic. The best of the best are the rich, deep green-blue colored French lentils—use with caution, though, as they're pretty addictive and a bit expensive. The regular ones are downright cheap, so they make great cost-effective meals.

1 small onion, finely chopped
5–6 cloves garlic, whole (peeled)
½ medium carrot, finely chopped
1 stalk of celery, finely chopped
1 or 2 bay leaves
3 cups (750 mL) lentils
1 Tbsp (15 mL) red wine vinegar
1–2 Tbsp (15–30 mL) olive oil
salt and pepper to taste

Throw all of the above ingredients into a pot. Add about 6 cups (1.5L) of water. Bring it to a boil, then reduce heat to medium, cover the pot and simmer on low-medium for a minimum of 30 minutes. The lentils should be tender. If you want to continue simmering, turn the heat down to low—the longer you cook lentils, the creamier they become. You can add more water if you want a brothier soup, then adjust the seasonings accordingly. Remove the bay leaves and serve.

This soup is wonderful left over. You can cook most of the liquid off, put it in the fridge, and then serve it cold as a spread or dip for crackers or bread.

I have yet to find lentils free of the odd tiny stone. Use a large white plate and put a handful of lentils at a time on it, sifting through with your fingers. If you find something smaller and darker than a lentil, pick it out. This is my method—if you have a better one, I'd love to hear about it!

Mega Minestrone

SERVES 6

Enjoy this hearty, traditional soup with family and friends. Your kitchen will smell fantastic! You can make this soup as rich or light as you like, or as mellow or spicy. I highly recommend that you double the recipe and keep the remainder in the fridge for lunches or freeze it for later.

½ cup (125 mL) zucchini, chopped
½ cup (125 mL) carrots, chopped
½ cup (125 mL) celery, chopped
½ cup (125 mL) green beans, chopped
3 cloves garlic, finely chopped
1 onion, finely chopped
1 tomato, chopped
½ cup (125 mL) cabbage, chopped
½ cup (125 mL) of canned cannellini, navy or lima beans
1 Tbsp (15 mL) tomato paste
1 Tbsp (15 mL) olive oil
about 4–5 cups (1.25 L) vegetable broth (or water), to cover
2 bay leaves
½ cup (125 mL) pasta (optional)
1 tsp (5 ml) oregano
1 tsp (5 mL) basil
salt and pepper to taste

Put all of the above ingredients into a large pot, except the pasta. You can add any other vegetables you have.

Bring it to a boil, then cover and let it simmer for at least 30 minutes. If the beans are dried, not canned, you can still do this the same way, but you'll have to increase the cooking time to at least an hour or more, depending on the beans.

About 10 minutes before serving the minestrone, turn up the heat to bring it to a boil, add the pasta, cover the pot, and cook to al dente (according to pasta package instructions). Scoop out the bay leaves. Remove it from the heat, add seasonings, and serve. Heavenly!

To keep your pasta al dente (firm), boil the pasta separately so you can add it to individual bowls. That way the remainder can be refrigerated or frozen without it.

Want a sophisto version? Add 2 cups (500 mL) of full-bodied red wine for part of the liquid, 2 Tbsp (30 mL) of capers, whole wheat pasta or 1 cup (250 mL) of cooked wild rice. Then throw on some finely shredded green onion to top it.

Blazing Sunset
Orange Ginger Broth

SERVES 4

Here's a wonderful prelude to an Asian meal. Serve it before some crispy spring rolls or a great stir-fry. Try it before a fall meal with root vegetables: potatoes, carrots, parsnips, turnips, beets, etc. This gingery, zingy broth is a perfect starter. Keep some in the fridge for a light lunch or snack. Get into the intense flavor and health benefits of eating ginger!

3 medium onions, finely chopped
1 Tbsp (15 mL) fresh, peeled, finely
    chopped ginger
3 cups (750 mL) orange juice
1 cup (250 mL) unsweetened soy milk
1 Tbsp (15 mL) orange zest
2 green onions, finely chopped
salt and pepper to taste

Put the onions and ginger in a pan with 1 cup (250 mL) of orange juice. Heat it to boiling and then reduce the heat to a simmer (medium-low).

When the onions are translucent, add the remainder of the orange juice, soy milk and salt and pepper. You can serve it almost immediately, but the flavors do blend better if you give the broth a bit of time to simmer (at least half an hour).

Strain out the ginger if you like—it can be hot. Just before serving, add the orange zest and green onion.

Remember getting ginger ale when you were sick as a kid? Ginger has historically been used to aid and calm digestion.

Puffy? There's a compound in ginger (oleoresins) that have anti-inflammatory properties.

Carsick? Bring a chunk of freshly cut ginger along for the ride. The scent of ginger is often used to treat nausea and helps some people beat motion sickness.

People know that orange juice contains vitamin C. But it also has calcium, folate, potassium, niacin, thiamine, vitamin B6, magnesium and natural antioxidants. Powerful!

Creamy Sunshine Corn Chowder

Creamy Sunshine Corn Chowder

SERVES 6

This is a great recipe for entertaining. You can put it on hours before your event, simmer it on low and forget about it, except for an occasional stir. It goes well with cornbread spiked with hot sauce or jalapeños, and an ultra crispy green salad.

3 cups (750 mL) fresh corn (kernels
    removed from cob)
½ large onion, finely diced
½ carrot, finely diced
1 medium potato, finely diced
1 stalk celery, finely diced
¼ cup (60 mL) green onion, finely chopped
½ cup (125 mL) fresh parsley, finely chopped
1 tsp (5 mL) turmeric or good pinch saffron
4 cups (1 L) unsweetened soy milk
salt and pepper to taste
3 cloves garlic, finely chopped (optional)

Simply place all of the above ingredients into a large pot and bring it to a boil. Reduce the heat to medium-low and simmer until the onion and potatoes are cooked (about 25–30 minutes). I like to remove about 1–2 cups (250–500 mL) of the chowder and blend it until creamy and smooth, then return it to the pot. This gives the chowder a velvety background, yet you still get whole pieces of corn, which is great. Take off the lid and gently simmer until lovely and thick, then serve.

The garlic is optional because while it is delicious, you may want to allow the sweet, fresh summer corn flavor to shine through. Save the delightful garlicky intensity for when you're using canned corn. You may want to reserve a bit of the green onion, or add extra, for sprinkling on the top when serving.

As for which to choose, turmeric or saffron, each complement the chowder with their yellow color and flavor. Saffron is more costly, though; in fact it's the most expensive spice in the world. The saffron threads are dried stigmas of the saffron flower (it's in the crocus family). It takes 75,000 flowers to produce a pound of saffron—wow. A little vial of the threads costs about $8–$10, so take your pick.

It's believed that the word chowder came from the word "chaudiere," which is the French word for a cauldron that fishermen used to cook up the catch of the day. There's also some speculation that the word "chowder" came from the word "chaud" (French for hot).

Mac's Chiller-Killer

SERVES 6–8

This insane combination of ingredients is sooo powerful for warming you up (mind, body and soul)! I highly recommend it. My husband, Mac, made this for me one night when I was freezing to death, and it was the perfect cure. If I'd known what was in it before I tasted it, I wouldn't have believed it could be so great.

If you don't have Jamaica Me Crazy, just add a few good shakes of coarse black pepper or ½ tsp (2 mL) of jerk sauce.

2 yellow potatoes, halved or
   quartered (Yukon Golds are great)
1 carrot, cut into 1–1½ inch lengths
1 leek, cut in half lengthwise,
   then cut into ½ inch pieces
2 medium onions, cut into quarters
8 cloves garlic, chopped
2 Tbsp (30 mL) balsamic vinegar
¼ cup (60 mL) rye whiskey
2 Tbsp (30 mL) soy sauce
2 Tbsp (30 mL) teriyaki sauce
2 Tbsp (30 mL) miso
1 cup (250 mL) dry, good red wine (Valpolicella is perfect)
½ tsp (2 mL) celery powder
½ tsp (2 mL) ground cloves
1 tsp (5 ml) seasoned pepper (Jamaica Me Crazy)
sea salt (to taste)
2 heaping tsp (10 mL) peanut butter (containing
   peanuts only)
2 tsp (10 mL) sesame oil
2 tsp (10 mL) dried basil
2 tsp (10 mL) fresh oregano leaves

Throw all of the ingredients into a large stockpot, then add water to cover. Bring it to a boil and then turn the heat down to low and simmer the soup, covered for 1 hour. Turn off the heat and let it rest for half an hour to allow flavors to really blend. Give it a mix, or reheat lightly, then serve. Yum! I'd love to hear if you find this as addictive as I do.

Carrots are common for starting a soup. Their sweetness adds a lot to the broth. Try a mirepoix for starting soup: a combo of about 50% onion, 25% celery and 25% carrots, all finely diced and sautéed at the beginning.

There are three kinds of miso: shiro (white), aka (red) and awase (blended). In general, shiro miso is somewhat sweeter. Aka miso is on the saltier side, although most are salty.

Mac makes soups that people go crazy over, and I mean they lose it! Once they taste them, they have to have more and more. These Mac-soups always have a wild amount of garlic and some kind of alcoholic beverage in them. He makes a bean soup I call "Mac's Magical Elixir"— it's not to be believed. (Yes, I will divulge it to you one day, when I figure it out!)

I wrote this recipe when I was dreaming of living in Palm Springs (which I intend to do). I just wanted to come up with something interesting and something I might want to eat on a winter's eve in the desert. I really liked the recipe when I tried it and I'll always be dreaming of PS when I eat it.

Put everything except the lasagna noodles, salt, pepper and avocados into a pot and cover it with water. Put a lid on it and simmer it until the vegetables are tender. I like to simmer this for at least an hour.

Then, bring the soup up to a full rolling boil and add the pasta. When it's almost done, add the salt and pepper. Remove the orange and lemon pieces and squeeze all the juice out of them, into the soup. Remove the bay leaves.

Peel and cut the avocados into bite-sized cubes and reserve.

Serve this in a beautiful shallow bowl, at just above room temperature, with a fully-loaded pepper grinder ready to go. Put some of the avocado cubes into each dish.

2 cloves garlic, finely chopped
1 whole orange, cut into quarters
1 whole lemon, cut into quarters
1 big chunk of ginger, scored so the flavor can seep out
4 green onions, finely chopped
1 red pepper, seeds removed and cut into rings
2 bay leaves
1 Tbsp (15 mL) light miso
6 sun-dried tomatoes, finely chopped
1 carrot, finely chopped
2 stalks celery, finely chopped
several basil leaves, finely chopped
½ cup flat-leaf parsley, finely chopped
1 tsp (5 mL) onion powder
1 tsp (5 mL) ground cumin
½ cup tomato sauce
4 whole wheat lasagna noodles, broken
salt and pepper to taste
2 avocados
1 finely chopped jalapeño pepper (if desired)

Jalapeños bespeak hot weather places and excitement. Have you ever had stuffed jalapeños? You can remove the seeds if you like it less heated, then stuff them with whatever tasty tidbits you like, and bake. They're wildly good—like a sunset in the desert.

When handling hot peppers, wear some gloves and keep your hands away from your face. I saw someone on TV the other day who was making the hottest curry on the planet, and if you walked into the kitchen while it was cooking, you had to wear a gas mask! Whoa.

We North Americans get most of our raw vegetables in salads. It's imperative to eat at least some raw foods. But all the washing and cutting up deters some people from making salad. Instead, they grab a convenience food. Let's face it—we're all busy. To make it as hassle-free as possible, you can do some of that washing and cutting when you bring the groceries home. It'll save you the time later when you're hungry.

Marinated artichokes, mushrooms or asparagus spears, a nice jar of roasted red peppers and a variety of olives are a few examples of some specialty items that can make your salads exciting. Nuts and seeds taste great and provide protein, fat and essential fatty acids. Cherry or grape tomatoes are quicker and more fun than having to wash and cut tomatoes. Use your imagination: baby corns, water chestnuts, cooked whole grains and green onions are just a few of the items you could sprinkle on top of your salad.

Seek out the best produce you can afford—check out organic markets and farmers' markets. Notice the difference in the crispness and flavor of the vegetables compared to those shipped across the world or sitting on a store shelf for a week (or much longer).

Experiment with salads and dressings. Always make them look beautiful—which is easy to do with all the colors—and have fun! Making salad should never be a chore, and eating salad should be one of the best parts of your day.

SEXY SALADS

Green, Green Salad

SERVES 6

A long time ago I was watching Julia Child on TV and a guest of hers prepared a salad that had only green things in it. Julia said something like: "My, that is unusual—usually there's a tomato or something of another color." The guest defended the "normal-ness" of the salad. It IS rather unusual to have an all-green salad though. (Julia was right, of course.) In the spirit of doing things differently, here's an all green salad for you. Hope ya love it.

1 head of crisp, leafy green lettuce
(romaine, green leaf or other)
1 bunch fresh spinach
2 green onions (green part only), finely chopped
1 cup (250 mL) flat-leaf parsley, finely chopped
sprig of fresh dill, finely chopped
1 green pepper, finely sliced into thin rings
⅓ cup (75 mL) extra virgin olive oil
¼ cup (60 mL) light vinegar
salt and pepper to taste

Wash the greens well. Dry the lettuce and spinach in a salad spinner or on paper towels. Remove any undesirable parts and spinach stems. Spinach leaves can stay whole, but rip or cut lettuce into bite-sized pieces. Add the other ingredients and drizzle the oil and vinegar over all. Normally I do half olive oil and half vinegar; I want the greenery here to be rich and glistening. Season your salad liberally with salt and pepper. You could add a squirt of lemon juice if you want extra tang. The onion and herbs provide amazing flavor. You can prepare everything earlier in the day; simply cover and refrigerate, then add the oil, vinegar, salt and pepper just before serving.

Simplicity at its best!

Julia Child (1912–2004) was a witty woman who introduced French cuisine to Americans in the '60s. She was a famous cook, author and TV personality. Her book *Mastering the Art of French Cooking* was a huge hit, as was her TV show "The French Chef." If you can see the old episodes of that show, by all means, do it. She was totally innovative with a great sense of humor.

These days it's trendy to put only one color of flower blooms into each vase. It's even more popular to do multiple vases, each with one different color. Why not do that with dishes? Try an all-green, all-orange or all-yellow dish to contrast other colorful foods.

Carrot-Lemon Zinger

SERVES 6

My mother-in-law makes a delicious version of this salad. It's one of my favorite dishes she makes—in a household of fabulous food. She grates the carrots and I don't think she puts any oil on it, but it's ultra-lemony and soooo refreshing. It's a bright and tasty side dish that's awesome at a formal dinner or a picnic.

5 carrots, peeled

1 fresh lemon, halved (for squirting)

salt to taste

drizzle extra virgin olive oil (optional)

fresh green herbs, finely chopped (optional)

Use a peeler (the German style swiveling head type works best). Make long, super-thin slices down the length of the carrot. It'll look like carrot fettuccine. You won't get right down to the exact center of the carrot without peeling your fingers, of course, but you can use the cores in a stock or somewhere else. Another option is to grate the carrots. Then, simply squeeze the lemon over the whole thing, salt, cover and refrigerate. When ready to serve, drizzle the oil and sprinkle fresh green herbs over it, if you like.

Green herbs are always tasty but there's a certain charm about the bright orange color of this salad alone. That goes double if you're serving it alongside something green. It's also good with a squirt of orange juice, in addition to the lemon, for a sweet zap. Delicious, fresh and jazzy—try it today.

Since the late 1980s, "baby carrots" have been a readily-available snack food. This is not a special variety of carrots at all—they're just regular carrots, cut up and then "tumbled" to round the edges. They have the charm of much smaller carrots. Most kids will eat these like candy.

Lemon juice is a terrific replacement for salt. Just like salt has that tang, lemon provides a different one, but equally delicious. And it brings out the flavors of other things and just kind of refreshes you all over.

Apollo Greek Salad

SERVES 4

This Greek salad is a gift from the gods with its celery, colorful peppers and various olives. I adore any Greek salad but the extras in this one make it much more fun. As for the dressing, this one is simple, and you could use any oil and vinegar combo with success.

½ cup (125 mL) kalamata olives
½ cup (125 mL) green olives
  (pimento-stuffed are fine)
1–2 stalks celery, chopped
2 bell peppers, chopped (any color)
2 tomatoes, chopped
1 red onion, chopped
1 cucumber, peeled and chopped (if organic,
  leave the peel on)
2 garlic cloves, finely chopped
1 tsp (5 mL) oregano
1 Tbsp (15 mL) fresh parsley, finely chopped
¼ cup (60 mL) extra virgin olive oil
¼ cup (60 mL) red wine vinegar
salt and pepper to taste
1 tsp (5 mL) capers (optional)

Put the above ingredients into a large bowl. Toss 'em well and let the salad sit for at least 5 minutes before serving to allow flavors to blend.

This is a perfect salad before pasta or any Mediterranean meal. On a hot summer night, this is the ultimate food to eat while lounging about, talking for hours with family and friends. Serve with a good red wine.

Traditionally, Greek salad has a slice of feta cheese, served on the side rather than totally laden with it, as is often seen. I would suggest even cheese eaters try it without—the flavors are amazing. It's a different experience.

A perfect addition to this is a spoonful of freshly chopped mint, which is also a traditional extra ingredient.

There is nothing more sublime to fill a wrap with than Greek salad. Simply fill in a line and roll it up. Chickpeas (or hummus) are a perfect addition and you can also use it as a sandwich filling with regular bread.

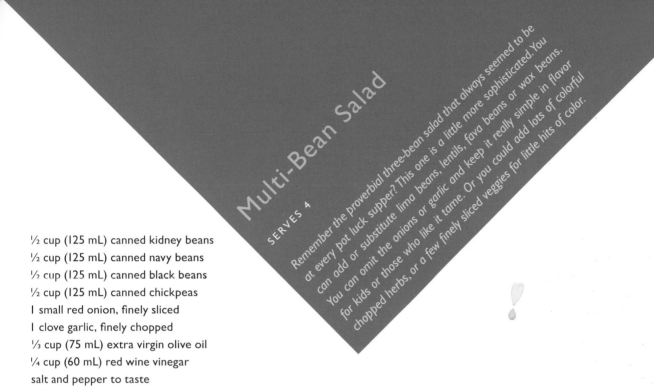

Multi-Bean Salad

SERVES 4

Remember the proverbial three-bean salad that always seemed to be at every pot luck supper? This one is a little more sophisticated. You can add or substitute lima beans, lentils, fava beans or wax beans. You can omit the onions or garlic and keep it really simple in flavor for kids or those who like it tame. Or you could add lots of colorful chopped herbs, or a few finely sliced veggies for little hits of color.

½ cup (125 mL) canned kidney beans
½ cup (125 mL) canned navy beans
½ cup (125 mL) canned black beans
½ cup (125 mL) canned chickpeas
1 small red onion, finely sliced
1 clove garlic, finely chopped
⅓ cup (75 mL) extra virgin olive oil
¼ cup (60 mL) red wine vinegar
salt and pepper to taste

Combine the above ingredients in a bowl and toss well.

Add 1 tsp (5 mL) of oregano, or ¼ cup (60 mL) of fresh, coarsely chopped basil leaves for some Mediterranean flair.

This makes a cool side dish any time of year, but it screams summer. It's delicious cold or at room temperature, but you could heat it too.

This would be nice alongside the Green, Green Salad (page 26) with a light pasta dish or rice pilaf.

Chickpeas, or garbanzo beans, are the most widely consumed legume on the planet. They're loaded with nutrition, including protein, phosphorus, calcium and iron. They're related to the green pea and are a wonderful addition to any diet.

Psychedelic Salad

SERVES 4

This salad looks gorgeous on a plate. It's vibrant, fresh, crunchy and good for you. The bright colors will captivate you before even taking a bite. You could cut the cabbage for easier eating but the charm of this is the big purple swirls at the bottom, with the other tidbits on top. Go for the gusto and use a knife and fork!

SALAD

1 whole small purple cabbage, sliced
   in rounds
1 green pepper, stemmed, seeded, cut in rings
1 small onion, ultra thinly sliced
1 large carrot, peeled and cut in matchsticks,
   or with a zigzag cutter
1 cup (250 mL) cherry or grape tomatoes
¼ cup (60 mL) fresh parsley or dill, finely chopped

DRESSING

¼ cup (60 mL) olive oil
¼ cup (60 mL) balsamic vinegar
1 clove garlic, finely chopped
salt and pepper to taste
1 green onion, finely chopped
½ cup (125 mL) finely chopped red pepper
1 Tbsp (15 mL) grated orange or lemon rind

FOR THE SALAD   Wash the entire head of cabbage, and then slice the whole thing as thinly as possible. You want ultra thin, large purple/white rounds of swirly color. Simply arrange them on the bottom of a large platter.

Next, sprinkle on the green pepper and onion, then the carrot and tomatoes. Finish with parsley or dill. A work of art!

FOR THE DRESSING   Whiz up the olive oil, vinegar, garlic, salt and pepper with a blender. Then stir in the green onion, red pepper and grated rind. Pour over the top for a beautiful result.

The smallest tomato species has tomatoes that are less than ¾ inch in diameter, and they come in yellow as well as red.

Here's something good to know: red bell peppers have 4 times the vitamin C of oranges.

Cabbage is rich in vitamin C and fiber. There's some evidence to suggest it reduces the chance of getting cancer, as evidenced in the Asian diet.

Psychedelic Salad

Sweet Cucumber Salad

This is the kind of sweet, refreshing salad that would be delicious alongside anything spicy. I've used it with curries, chili and when the table just looks like it needs one more dish but I don't feel like doing anything complex. Kids are usually crazy about this because of the sweetness.

2–3 cucumbers, preferably
 long English, but any will do
I tsp (5 mL) sugar or honey†
I Tbsp (15 mL) apple cider vinegar

Seed the cucumbers by cutting them lengthwise and scooping out the seeds with a spoon. This is completely a matter of personal preference. (There are people who'll feel ripped off if the seeds are missing!)

Cut the cucumbers into the absolute thinnest slices you possibly can. If you have a mandolin or one of those crazy slicers that you have to use a protective device with so you don't slice off your fingers, use that. Place the sliced cucumbers in a bowl and add the other ingredients. Stir well. Let it sit at least 5 minutes before serving.

† VEGAN OPTION agave syrup, brown rice syrup or barley malt syrup

Cool as a cucumber? Cucumbers do have wonderful cooling properties and make perfect summer salads and refreshers alongside spicy dishes.

Ever had Japanese cucumbers? They're very similar to the long English cucumbers, but they have prickly skin.

Cucumbers are actually members of the gourd family. They originate from India, and were adored by ancient Greeks and Romans.

Two famous cucumber dishes are raita (Indian) and tzatziki (Greek). Both are cucumber with yogurt and seasonings, used as condiments and totally delicious. Some vegans make these with soy yogurt as a base; I prefer to do it with puréed white bean.

Celery Refresher

Sometimes you just need a salad with some severe crunch. I like to serve more full-bodied salads like this with a soup or with anything that doesn't have a crunchy texture to it.

4 stalks celery, washed, ends
   and strings removed
2 carrots, peeled
1 large tomato
small bit of extra firm lettuce (the heart is best)
1 stalk broccoli
1 red onion (optional)
½ cup (125 mL) extra virgin olive oil
¼ cup (60 mL) red wine or balsamic vinegar
½ tsp (2 mL) basil, oregano or both
salt and pepper to taste

Chop all of the above into bite-sized pieces. Place in a large bowl and dress with oil, vinegar and seasonings. Let it sit for about 20 minutes for flavors to meld. I like this salad to be crisp, fresh and simple. You could add extra seasonings if you wish. I know this is pretty basic but there are times in life when you don't want to fuss.

This is a good year-round salad. You can probably get these ingredients even in the dead of winter. (Okay, the tomato won't get any awards, unless you live somewhere hot.) It's great as a meal with some light sandwiches or as a preview to some steaming hot, creamy soup on a freezing day.

Although celery is very low in calories (around 10 calories per medium stalk), it contains potassium, vitamin C and a bit of dietary fiber. Plus it adds flavor and crunch to all kinds of dishes.

Why cry over onions? Because they contain sulphuric compounds, that's why. If you chill them, it helps somewhat.

Killer Tomato Salad

This is the ultimate salad for tomato lovers. You need wonderful, ripe tomatoes to really do it justice. If you're a gardener, this recipe is perfect to showcase those homegrown beauties. This simple salad packs huge flavor—like taking a bite of pure sunshine.

5 large, ripe, red tomatoes
½ cup (125 mL) extra virgin olive oil
¼ cup (60 mL) balsamic vinegar
a good, big bunch of fresh basil
sea salt to taste

Slice the tomatoes in large rounds at least ¼ inch (6 mm) thick and arrange them on a large platter. Drizzle with the oil and vinegar. Chop the basil coarsely or just tear the leaves up and sprinkle them over the top, so that each piece has some basil. Season the whole thing with sea salt (I prefer the coarse one here, but use what you love).

Serve immediately. This is perfect before any Mediterranean-style meal, before a pasta course (I would present this before a pasta dish that won't have tomato sauce, for contrast) or before something deliciously grilled.

This dish IS summer. It's fantastic eaten outside with a huge goblet of dry, red wine. If you're drinking water, embellish it with a lime wedge for fun.

Basil is native to tropical parts of Asia and India. It's a star of Thai, Vietnamese and Italian cuisines. It's a fantastic herb with a ton of versatility.

I have made this dish with some chilled, roasted green peppers alternating between the tomato slices. A beautiful garnish for the center of the plate is a little pile of pine nuts with a sprig of basil poking out of the top.

If you don't have the fresh basil, still make this dish with dried. It's not the same, but it's great in a completely different way.

Waldorf Salad Nouveau

SERVES 4

The weird and wonderful Waldorf Salad was a staple at buffets during the '60s and '70s, but has since kind of fallen out of fashion. I'm not the type who would normally put celery into a fruity dish, but it really works. Make sure you use ultra crisp celery. As for the apples, try any kind you like. I adore Granny Smith apples, but I like to throw a red one in for the color, leaving the skins on.

3 ripe, firm apples, cubed or sliced
1 large stalk celery, finely diced
½ cup (125 mL) extra virgin olive oil
6–8 whole walnuts or pecans
½ cup (125 mL) coarsely chopped walnuts
   or pecans
1 tsp (5 mL) lemon juice
pinch brown sugar (optional)
lettuce to serve on (butter or iceberg lettuces are great)
½ cup (125 mL) dried cranberries
salt and pepper to taste

Combine the apples and celery. In a separate bowl, put the olive oil, 3 or 4 walnuts or pecans, lemon juice and sugar (if desired). Blend the ingredients with an upright or hand blender until the mixture reaches the consistency of mayonnaise. Pour it over the apple/celery mixture and chill well.

Add ½ cup (125 mL) of chopped walnuts or pecans just before serving and stir in. Use any additional whole nuts to garnish the salad, along with celery leaves if desired. Place on a crispy lettuce bed or you could serve this salad in cored out apples—it looks wild! Sprinkle dried cranberries over the top.

Oscar Tschirky, maître d'hôtel of New York's famed Waldorf-Astoria Hotel, created the Waldorf Salad in 1896. Originally, it consisted of apples, celery and mayonnaise and was a huge hit. Chopped walnuts were added later. It's usually served atop a bed of lettuce.

If you have leftover Waldorf Salad Nouveau, here's an idea. Throw it into a pan with some curry powder, salt, pepper and a bit of soy milk or water so it doesn't stick. Toss it around in the pan on medium-high heat until the curry smells wonderful and it's hot and bubbly. Put it over rice and it's really differently delicious.

Try the idea for this salad as a jumping-off point to create something similar using different fruits. A Pear Waldorf would be magnificent!

Coleslaw Divine

This version is fresh and delicious, packed with flavor and better without the dairy products. I keep some chopped cabbage in the fridge so I can make it in a flash if I don't feel like cutting! It's quick and cabbage is great for you. Try some soon.

2 cups (500 mL) cabbage
   (green, purple, or both) finely sliced
½ cup (125 mL) shredded or grated carrot
¼ cup (60 mL) shredded red onion (optional)
2 Tbsp (30 mL) olive oil
1 Tbsp (15 mL) apple cider vinegar
2 tsp (10 mL) Dijon mustard
1 clove garlic, finely chopped
salt and pepper to taste
1–2 tsp honey† (optional)
any additional herbs you wish to add (fresh dill, basil,
   parsley or crisp, chopped celery leaves are great)

Put the cabbage into a bowl. You can buy pre-shredded cabbage—it works for a busy schedule. Or you can cut it finely with a big knife, or shred it in a food processor. I like to do a similar mix to the kind in the store: mostly green, with perhaps a 1:10 combo of purple cabbage and carrots. For a treat, use a savoy cabbage (the finer, crinkly variety). It makes a nice change from the average.

In a separate bowl, mix the remaining ingredients together, and then add them to your cabbage bowl. Toss it really well. Taste and adjust accordingly. Try a different salad dressing for a change of pace.

† VEGAN OPTION agave syrup, brown rice syrup or barley malt syrup

Babe Ruth is said to have put a cabbage leaf under his hat during his baseball games, trading it for a fresh one halfway through.

Captain Cook knew of sauerkraut's medicinal value way back in 1769. His ship's doctor made compresses for wounded soldiers with the brine, to prevent gangrene. The value of eating cultured vegetables, like sauerkraut, is becoming popular again, as their health benefits are becoming more widely recognized.

Cabbage contains an antioxidant called quercetin. It's said to be a natural antihistamine and may provide relief to some people with allergies.

No Wilt Salad

This is a wonderful year-round salad. I love to serve this chilled on a hot evening or as a light meal in autumn. It's fun to serve a couple of different dressings in mini cups on each plate for dipping. It's also a perfect lunch-on-the-go.

½ cup (125 mL) broccoli, cut finely

½ cup (125 mL) carrots, cut into matchsticks

½ cup (125 mL) cauliflower, finely sliced

½ cup (125 mL) red onion, finely chopped or sliced

½ red pepper, finely sliced in rings or pieces

½ cup (125 mL) slivered almonds

½ cup (125 mL) green beans†

3 Tbsp (45 mL) extra virgin olive oil

2 Tbsp (30 mL) red wine vinegar

1 garlic clove, crushed

salt and pepper to taste

Combine and toss all of the ingredients. Let the salad sit for a few minutes before serving. If you want something really low-cal, you can omit the olive oil. Drizzle a little good soy sauce over the salad and add a squirt of lime juice instead. You could always add some finely chopped herbs of your choice.

† Use fresh green beans that have been lightly blanched for a minute or so in boiling water and then chilled. Or you can use thawed frozen green beans.

This salad is insanely good with curry on it. Just make any dressing you like and add ½ tsp (2 mL) of any variety of curry powder into it for a light curry flavor. If you were to make a big batch of this, you could eat it hot one day, cold another.

For speed, you could slice all these ingredients in a food processor. Then you could dress your gourmet slaw with a decadent dressing like Glamorous Green Goddess (page 54) and pack it for a perfect picnic lunch with some bread on the side.

Another way to spin this salad into something new is to add a lot of peeled, cut orange and grapefruit slices. Blood oranges would be nice with their deep color. Add extra almonds if you decide to try this—they're amazing with oranges.

Brilliant Beet Salad

The wild and wicked color of beets is perfect to jazz up any table. If you're like I was and had only tasted pickled beets, try them in their unpickled state. They're yummy: sweet, sometimes a little tart—an earthy root vegetable.

bunch of beets (about 6 or so)
1–2 Tbsp (15–30 mL) extra virgin olive oil
2 tsp (10 mL) apple cider vinegar
1 Tbsp (15 mL) grated orange rind
½ cup (125 mL) fresh parsley, finely chopped
1 green onion, coarsely chopped
salt and pepper to taste

Although this is how I cook beets, I'm sure it's not the proper way (not that I've ever checked). I tried once to cut off the skin of a raw beet and found it was too much of a hassle. Life's too short. So here goes: boil up a big pot of water. Give the beets a quick wash, just to make sure they're free of dirt. Put them into the boiling water, including the beet greens if you have them.

If you do have the greens, remove them from the pot as soon as they're a bright green. The beets aren't done until you can poke a fork right into them (about 25–30 minutes) depending on the size. When fork-tender, remove them and cool them. At that point, simply run the beets under cool water, give them a push with your fingers and the skin will slide right off. Any picky parts and ends can easily be cut off.

Slice the beets or leave any tiny ones whole. Dress them with the olive oil and vinegar. Sprinkle on the grated orange rind, parsley and green onion. Taste and season accordingly.

If you don't feel like boiling beets, you can do this with canned or jarred ones.

Reserve a bit of the beet juice and refrigerate it in an airtight container. Use it for food coloring, to make delightful reddish-purple embellishments on all kinds of things—it's perfect for icings. You can make light pinkish-purple to more intense colors, and it's all perfectly natural.

Many cultures swear by the healing power of beets. They're used to treat many ailments, including bladder problems, constipation, even cancer.

Even though beets have the highest sugar content of any vegetable, they're low in calories and help rid the body of fatty deposits.

TOP Brilliant Beet Salad MIDDLE Green, Green Salad (page 26) BOTTOM Carrot-Lemon Zinger (page 27)

Sweet Corn and Spelt Dinner Salad

SERVES 4

Here's a dinner that's refreshing on the hottest of days, but filling enough to get you through the night. This is a perfect example of the glory of whole grains, as well as eating in season.

4 ears of gorgeous corn on
   the cob, husked
2 cups (500 mL) spelt, cooked
2 cups (500 mL) cherry or grape tomatoes
2 small zucchinis, cut into rounds
1 cup (500 mL) baby carrots, cut into quarters
¼ cup (60 mL) chives, cut into about 1 inch pieces
4 cups (1 L) arugula or baby spinach leaves
½ cup (125 mL) fresh mint, finely chopped
½ cup (125 mL) flat-leaf parsley, coarsely chopped
drizzle of your best extra virgin olive oil
drizzle of rice vinegar
sprinkling of coarse sea salt
freshly cracked pepper

Put a pot of water on the stove to boil. When it's at a full, rolling boil, add the corn. Boil for 3½ minutes. Believe it or not, that's enough time to cook out the harsh part of the starch and bring up the color. Remove them from the heat and pop the corn into an ice water bath. When they're cool, remove and cut the kernels off with a sharp knife. They'll come off in strips and some will stay together, which is fine.

Put the corn into a large bowl, add the other ingredients—except the salt and pepper—and toss it well. Cover and wait about 10 minutes before tasting, allowing time for the flavors to blend. Then taste and add salt and pepper only if desired. It depends on the variety of corn you use. If it's ultra-sweet, you might want more, less or no salt and pepper at all.

Serve this on a beautiful plate and eat outside if at all possible. This is a complete meal—very satisfying and tasty.

There's a blue variety of corn, often used in making blue corn chips (they actually look more purple). Blue chips are gorgeous served with salsa, because of the wild color.

The zucchini flower is the preferred part of the plant in Mexican cooking. It's used in soups and quesadillas.

How sad: many people have never tried raw zucchini. It's delicious just sliced up into rounds and served with a dip. Call 'em zucchini chips—kids who would never accept cooked zucchini might go for it raw.

Top-Notch Pasta Salad

These pasta salads replace the boring macaroni salad of old: the elbow macaroni, the tame ingredients, the salad dressing or mayo. My pasta salads are pretty popular, and here I give you the keys to making amazing ones.

Start with a pasta shape you love and make sure it's cooked al dente. If you're going to a party, make enough to fill a deep-dish casserole or lasagna pan. Drizzle the pasta with extra virgin olive oil and toss it well. Once in a blue moon, I'll substitute it with, or add, pure sesame oil or flaxseed oil.

I always like to add an acid (just like in a regular salad dressing). You can squirt it with any citrus fruit juice. Lemon's always a hit. If you want it to have a more Mexican flair, go for the lime. If you're going in the Italian direction, perhaps some wine vinegar or balsamic will be your choice; for an Asian-inspired salad, maybe a rice vinegar. You could also use a drizzle of wine instead of vinegar.

I like to use equal amounts of vegetables and pasta. So, if I use 1 cup (250 mL) of pasta, then I'll add 1 cup (250 mL) of chopped vegetables.

From this point on, the choices are endless. Use some or all of the following ideas; use whatever you have on hand, or whatever you love.

*Top-Notch Pasta Salad Variations
on the following page . . .*

Top-Notch Pasta Salad Variations

PASTA SALAD ITALIANO   Use roasted red peppers, capers, marinated mushrooms, olives, slivered onions, tons of finely chopped garlic, fresh basil, artichokes, tomatoes, green peppers, pine nuts, spinach, dried rosemary, oregano and lots of black pepper. Garnish with large tomato circles with a black olive in the middle of each and a full bunch of chopped flat-leaf parsley.

CHOPSTICK PASTA SALAD   Use water chestnuts, bamboo shoots, baby corns, shiitake or oyster mushrooms (you can quickly stir-fry these in a bit of soy sauce and garlic first for an added flavor dimension), lots of chopped green onion, finely chopped garlic, fresh or powdered ginger, soy or teriyaki sauce, chopped peppers, onions and white pepper.

SHADES OF INDIA PASTA SALAD   Use finely chopped greens, spinach, cilantro, chopped tomato, lots of chopped onions, finely sliced cucumber, a bit of cubed, cooked potato, some grated carrot, curry powder or paste, some fennel seeds, a pinch of cloves, ground cumin, a bit of ginger, hot curry or hot sauce and dried fruit.

GORGEOUS GREEK PASTA SALAD   Use Kalamata olives, lots of sliced red onion, lots of chopped tomato, some chunky cucumber, a good sprinkle of oregano, a pinch of cinnamon, lemon juice and a bit of zested lemon rind. Coarse salt is great here too.

EASY YUMMY PICNIC PASTA SALAD   Use finely chopped carrots, finely chopped celery, a bit of finely chopped onion, salt, pepper and a pinch each of onion powder and paprika. Try the traditional elbow macaroni shape here, maybe with whole wheat pasta instead of white. It's easy, but great.

DIVE INTO THE GARLIC PASTA SALAD   Use a bulb (or more) of roasted garlic, a bulb (or more) of fresh garlic, finely chopped, a little celery, tomato and chopped parsley for color. Some fine little lemon slices would be pretty here too. A good sprinkling of coarse sea salt finishes it.

ONION LOVERS PASTA SALAD Cook a variety of chopped onions in a little bit of olive oil and white wine. Some green onions, white onions, red onions and even some shallots, all finely chopped or sliced would be perfection. Add to the pasta of your choice; bows or shells would be fun. A good dose of salt and pepper, and some chopped carrots and celery and this would be to die for.

SPRING PASTA SALAD Use light spring onions, sliced lengthwise, fresh light baby greens, baby carrots finely sliced, some baby organic peas or better yet, snow peas. Add some grated lemon and orange rinds and juice, keeping it all lively and light.

SUMMER PASTA SALAD Go for the bounty of the season here. Thickly chopped, red ripe tomatoes, summer peas, sweet corn, some chopped sweet or ultra dilly pickles, firm cucumbers and anything else gorgeous and garden-fresh. Vegetable flavors will star so you won't need much seasoning.

FALL PASTA SALAD Use any steamed or lightly cooked root vegetables—parsnips, carrots, beets, rutabagas, turnips, Brussels sprouts, chopped acorn or butternut squash, fresh or dried sage or savory (stuffing-like, thinking about Thanksgiving and the first frost), a bit of parsley, onions, salt, pepper. If you use, say, a raw parsnip (you'll usually find them cooked), it would be best to finely shred or grate it. Use your discretion and if you think something should be cooked, give it a steaming.

WINTER PASTA SALAD Get whatever's in season in your part of the world, or use frozen. Use plenty of garlic and robust flavors; you could add some canned beans, corn, parsley, onions or anything that strikes you. Maybe make it spicier than usual to shake you out of a winter chill.

Enjoy! Be the hit of the party while remembering two things: if you make a particularly fab pasta salad, write it down because six months later, someone will ask for the recipe (and it will be gone unless you have a killer memory). Also, everyone will love it and want you to bring it forever more.

I love dressings! Great dressings make great salads. I could eat a salad for almost every meal, but not with some non-fat, store-bought dressing. Ick! Read the ingredients: *most* are brutally gross. Many are full of chemicals, or garbage oils, and they never taste like anything real.

Dressing is so important to a salad. You can use any dressing you like on these salads. I've included these to spark your imagination: I want you to be crazy about making fresh dressings and I want you to go wild for salads. No matter what your diet, if you add a quality salad to every meal, you can change your physiology.

If you're going to use low-fat or non-fat dressing, it's best made fresh. When I say fresh, you don't have to make it that second; most can be stored in the fridge for about 5 days.

Olive oil, like all oils, is 100% fat, so if fat content is an issue, use it sparingly. However, there are health benefits to using olive oil in reasonable amounts, as evidenced in the Mediterranean diet. My attitude is if I'm eating a salad as a meal, then I can have extra virgin olive oil on it. You don't need much for richness, just a drizzle. If you don't use oil, however, you'll need intensely zingy flavor.

To make a basic dressing, take one part oil (I vote for olive) and, say, another part acid (vinegar, wine, fruit juice, etc.). Then add *any* seasonings you like. Or play with those amounts. Go for a walk on the wild side—add something unexpected.

The dressings I've included here are mostly updated versions of fairly traditional ones. I want you to have some good base dressings. Play with flavors: sweet, salty, hot, tangy—you'll come up with some wild ones.

SUPERIOR SALAD DRESSINGS

Oil and Vinegar Italiano

MAKES 1 CUP

This dressing is an impeccable preview to a spicy spaghetti dinner. Or use it to dress something you've just cooked and already doused in garlic—this dressing is also just as wonderful without the garlic. Don't be confined by any of the recipes; you won't ruin them if you rework them! It's all a matter of taste.

½ cup (125 mL) red wine vinegar
½ cup (125 mL) extra virgin olive oil
1 tsp (5 mL) basil (dried, or fresh
    and finely cut)
1 tsp (5 mL) oregano (dried, or fresh
    and finely cut)
1 clove garlic, finely diced
salt and pepper to taste

Combine the above ingredients and shake it in a covered container or simply whisk it together. Let it sit, covered, for about an hour before serving to allow the flavors to meld.

This dressing can be used as a marinade for any savory dish you bake or barbecue.

In Italy, a pre-made vinaigrette for salad is rarely seen. Usually olive oil, vinegar, salt and pepper are served at the table and everyone adds their own as they wish.

You can switch this dressing to a "Creamy Italiano" by adding 2 Tbsp (30 mL) pine nuts, then puréeing it with an upright or hand blender.

If you want a fat-free version, use veggie broth instead of the oil. Then season it a little stronger than you normally would.

Try this dressing on a salad of radicchio, thinly sliced cucumber, slivered onions and some olives. It's wonderful.

Nectar-with-a-Sting Honey Mustard

There's nothing like a little honey mustard dressing to liven up a summer lunch or wake up a plain ol' baked potato. This is a beautiful dressing on butter lettuce. The delicate leaves work perfectly with this sweet and tart dressing.

1 Tbsp (15 mL) Dijon
  (or other mustard)
1 Tbsp (15 mL) honey†
2 Tbsp (30 mL) extra virgin olive oil
2 tsp (10 mL) apple cider vinegar
1 clove garlic, minced
salt and pepper to taste

Blend all the ingredients with an upright or hand blender. Or shake well in a covered container.

Most people love the flavor of honey combined with the zap of mustard. You can make it sweeter or tangier, as you wish. A heavy cream consistency is great for this dressing but if you want it thinner, add a little more vinegar.

† VEGAN OPTION agave syrup, brown rice syrup or barley malt syrup

Most of the mustard seeds used in Dijon, France are grown in Canada and the United States. About 90% of the world's mustard seeds are produced in Canada.

More than 1,600 gallons plus 2,000,000 individual packets of mustard are consumed at New York's Yankee Stadium in a single year.

Honey contains the vitamins B6, thiamin, niacin, riboflavin and pantothenic acid.

Agave syrup is from the agave cactus plant in Mexico. It has a glycemic index of 46, making it more easily tolerated by diabetics than some other sugars.

Supreme Toasted Sesame Dressing

This dressing is really intense in flavor. If you love the toasty taste of sesame seeds, this dressing will become a favorite.

½ cup (125 mL) extra virgin olive oil
1 Tbsp (15 mL) toasted sesame oil
1 Tbsp (15 mL) toasted sesame seeds
1 clove garlic, finely minced
½ cup (125 mL) rice vinegar (or other light vinegar)
1 green onion, ultra finely chopped
salt and pepper to taste

You can buy toasted sesame seeds, but if you have the raw variety, it's simple to toast them. Put them into a dry pan, on medium heat and keep the pan moving until they heat up. You'll smell the toasty sesame fragrance (heaven!), then heat a few seconds more, keeping the pan moving. Remove from the heat and transfer to another container to stop the cooking process.

Combine the olive oil, toasted sesame oil, sesame seeds, rice vinegar and garlic and blend until smooth. Add the green onion, taste, and add salt and pepper to taste.

Try this over fresh lettuce, chopped with bean sprouts and a few water chestnuts. It's also great on any greens and tomato salad. It works as an ultra yummy stir-fry sauce or to drizzle over rice, grains or veggies. It's perfect with tempeh and veggies on a skewer—brush on beforehand and save some to dip into.

Add a dash of soy sauce to boost the flavor! Only a dash though—this dressing is so sublime, you won't want to go too far off the sesame track.

You can marinate roasted peppers in this dressing and they'll be incredible to serve plain or on crackers.

If you like hot stuff, mix ½ tsp (2 mL) of wasabi powder (Japanese horseradish) into this for something pizzazzy.

Citrus-Hit Dressing

This is a wonderfully tangy dressing. It's perfect for when you're making a heavy meal and want something light to complement it. You could make some just because you want to liven up your taste buds.

1 Tbsp (15 mL) lemon rind, finely grated
1 Tbsp (15 mL) lime rind, finely grated
1 Tbsp (15 mL) orange rind, finely grated
⅓ cup (75 mL) fresh lemon juice
⅓ cup (75 mL) fresh lime juice
⅓ cup (75 mL) fresh orange juice
1 cup (250 mL) extra virgin olive oil
1 mint leaf, finely chopped
1 lemon basil leaf, finely chopped
salt and pepper to taste
pulp from any citrus fruits above (optional)
1 teaspoon honey† (optional)

Blend up the citrus juices and grated rinds (zest). Add the oil slowly and blend it well; use as much as you like for balance. Add the mint, lemon basil, salt and pepper and stir well. This may be too much dressing for you to use right away, but just cover and refrigerate it; it'll keep for at least a couple of weeks in the fridge (the ascorbic acid from the fruit extends the life of this dressing).

This is good with delicate baby lettuces and butter lettuce. It's incredible brushed onto kabobs or drizzled over grain dishes. It's a great idea to keep some on hand—you'll certainly find endless uses for it.

† **VEGAN OPTION** agave syrup, brown rice syrup or barley malt syrup

To create a great fruit salad, try this dressing on a variety of fresh fruits, but leave out the oil. In addition to tasting terrific, all that citrus juice helps to keep fruits from turning brown.

Grate or zest as much rind as you can out of the peel, with as little of the white pith as possible (it can be bitter). Of course, if you don't have the lemon basil, use regular basil or leave it out. The mint is a really nice touch. Don't worry if you don't get the full amount of rind off the fruits—just add what you can remove.

Infinity Dressing

The wondrous thing about this dressing is that it can be used in so many (infinite) ways. It's a great dressing or marinade for almost anything. Drizzle some over grain dishes, use it to brush on foods you're grilling and keep some on hand for whatever comes up.

¼ cup (60 mL) extra virgin olive oil
¼ cup (60 mL) soy sauce
¼ cup (60 mL) apple cider vinegar
2 tsp (10 mL) honey†

Mix the above together well with a whisk, or put it in a covered container and shake it. This makes a good dressing or dipping sauce for fresh, crisp vegetables of all kinds. It works as a great stir-fry sauce. My kids will eat endless amounts of cucumbers with this dressing, with or without the honey.

Use it to drizzle over anything piping hot out of the oven or for a marinade for veggies that you're going to skewer, or for tempeh or a casserole. It's great for complementing Chinese food and terrific with steamed vegetables.

† VEGAN OPTION agave syrup, brown rice syrup or barley malt syrup

The "dosage" of organic apple cider vinegar is 2 Tbsp in 8 oz of liquid, 3 times a day. It's said to improve circulation and joint problems, and give energy and refreshed skin. There are all kinds of other positive claims as well.

This is yet another dressing that's good to serve in a small bowl on a large plate. It's perfect for dipping practically anything, so may go with the entire meal.

Try adding a couple of spoons of this to any casserole you're baking—it adds extra zip.

Billion Island Dressing

I always thought Thousand Island dressing had an odd taste, but so many people love it. Other than the killer sweetness, it never seems to have enough flavor. For a more cultured kick, try this new non-dairy version of the standard Thousand Island dressing:

¼ cup (60 mL) extra virgin olive oil
½ cup (125 mL) lemon juice or vinegar
2 cloves garlic, finely minced
1 tsp (5 mL) honey†
1 tsp (5 mL) soy sauce
1 tsp (5 mL) tomato paste
1 tsp (5 mL) prepared mustard
salt and pepper to taste
½ tsp (2 mL) paprika
1 Tbsp (15 mL) dill pickle finely chopped
1 Tbsp (15 mL) celery, finely chopped
1 Tbsp (15 mL) parsley, finely chopped
cayenne pepper to taste (optional)
dash of dry sherry to taste (optional)

Blend everything except the pickle, celery and parsley. Then add them in and stir well. This dressing is good for hearty, leafy green salads. You can also use it as a dip for cut up vegetables.

If you're a gardener with access to fresh herbs, make this one for sure. This dressing brings vitality to salads or to whatever you serve it with.

† VEGAN OPTION agave syrup, brown rice syrup or barley malt syrup

Thousand Island is a variation on Russian dressing that had a yogurt base with chili sauce or ketchup. The early Thousand Island dressing had a mayo base with pickle relish, chopped, hard-boiled eggs and chives. In the '50s it was popular in sandwiches and salads, made with mayo, ketchup and pickle relish.

You can use this as a dip, but what's even better is to add some pureed vegetable (potato, carrot, etc.) to it to give it more body.

Here's something deliciously different. Try some garlicky marinated oyster mushrooms and barbecue them. Then use this as a dipping sauce on the side.

Frisky French Dressing

This is a simple French style dressing that's kind of all-purpose. You can use it for almost any salad with great success, especially for those who aren't as adventurous in the dressing department. It has a lot of flavor, with that traditional edge that makes it a favorite.

½ cup (125 mL) extra virgin olive oil
¼ cup (60 mL) lemon juice or vinegar
1 tsp (5 mL) honey†
1 tsp (5 mL) tomato paste
1 tsp (5 mL) Dijon mustard
1 clove garlic, finely minced
salt and pepper to taste

Blend up the above ingredients until everything's as smooth as silk.

For a nice variation on the above, make Roasted Red Pepper French. Prepare it the same way, but replace the tomato paste with about ¼ cup (60 mL) of roasted red peppers. The roasted pepper is soft enough to blend nicely.

Either one of these will make an iceberg lettuce and tomato salad a much jazzier experience.

† VEGAN OPTION agave syrup, brown rice syrup or barley malt syrup

It's said that Lucious French, one of the founders of Hazelton, Indiana, hated his veggies. Supposedly, his wife created the dressing to entice him into eating them.

In Biloxi, Mississippi, they pour French Dressing on pizza! (Hmmm, sounds kinda good…)

You can spin this into a "Creamy French" by whizzing in a few white beans, some roasted garlic or a bit of unsweetened soy milk.

LEFT TO RIGHT Billion Island Dressing (page 51), Oil and Vinegar Italiano (page 46), Citrus-Hit Dressing (page 49), Rich Roasted Garlic Dressing (page 57), Glamorous Green Goddess (page 54), Frisky French Dressing (page 52)

Glamorous Green Goddess

This dressing is smooth and green. Chill it to serve as a cool dip on a hot summer's day—all that fresh green will energize your spirit and tantalize your taste buds.

2 green onions, chopped

½ cup (125 mL) fresh parsley, chopped

½ cup (125 mL) fresh basil, chopped

½ cup (125 mL) fresh dill, chopped

½ cup (125 mL) spinach

more fresh green herbs, if you have them on hand

½ cup (125 mL) medium tofu

1 Tbsp (15 mL) lemon or lime juice

1 Tbsp (15 mL) extra virgin olive oil

salt and pepper to taste

For increased texture, reserve a bit of the herbs to chop finely and add in at the end. Otherwise, simply combine the above ingredients and blend until smooth. Check for seasonings and adjust them accordingly.

This dressing is amazing on a salad of fresh red peppers and cucumbers, finely sliced or cut small. It's also great on butter lettuce. Try it on a variety of different salads to see what you come up with. It makes a colorful party dip too.

William Archer, the playwright, had a hit play called *The Green Goddess*. Apparently the head chef of the Palace Hotel in San Francisco in the '20s wanted to recognize this and did so with his creation, Green Goddess Dressing. It became a huge hit on the West coast.

Although the base for Green Goddess dressing is usually mayonnaise and/or sour cream, some great alternatives are tahini or any white bean.

Gorgeous Greek Marinade/Dressing

This could be called Instant Greek because anything you put it on will have the flavor of Greece. Try this the next time you barbecue—it makes a terrific marinade.

1 cup (250 mL) extra virgin
   olive oil
½ cup (125 mL) fresh lemon juice
4 cloves garlic, finely chopped
1 Tbsp (15 mL) oregano
½ tsp (2 mL) salt
½ tsp (2 mL) pepper

Blend the above ingredients smoothly or coarsely depending on your needs. Silky smooth is nice if you're putting this on a salad. If you're using it as a marinade, the garlic is good a little chunky.

Use this to marinade tofu, or vegetables to skewer, to drizzle over salads, beans and fresh, crisp vegetables. It rocks as a flavoring for cooking rice dishes, for pasta, pizza and just about anything else.

Cut up a bunch of potatoes into nice, thick wedges. Put them into a large lasagna pan with a couple of cut up onions. Pour this dressing over the top, give it a toss and bake in a 350°F (180°C) oven for about 1 hour or more, turning occasionally. To make it even better, add some white wine along the way. Ta da—Greek roasted potatoes!

If you have some beautiful, fresh, finely chopped mint, that would be a great replacement for the oregano. Or use some in addition to the oregano for another layer of flavor. For a completely different, but equally delicious dressing, instead of the garlic use a lot of super finely chopped chives.

Super Faux Caesar Dressing

This is a really cool recipe because it's a way of getting flaxseeds into your diet.

This dressing is perfect on a traditional romaine lettuce salad. If you like flaxseeds, you can add extra on top, and maybe you'd like to add some croutons for a little more crunch. If your lettuce is ultra crisp, that'll be enough texture, with this rich, creamy dressing.

1 cup (250 mL) best extra virgin
    olive oil
½ cup (125 mL) light vinegar
2 Tbsp (30 mL) flaxseeds
3 cloves garlic, chopped
salt and pepper to taste

Combine the above ingredients and blend until smooth.

This is a surprisingly delicious dressing. You may also enjoy this as a decadent dip for celery or carrot sticks.

Flaxseeds contain lignans, which the National Cancer Institute acknowledges as having certain cancer-fighting capabilities.

The Omega-3 in 3 lb of salmon is the same as 50 grams of flaxseeds—these fatty acids help prevent heart disease.

Flax is high in fiber and there's evidence that it's helpful to skin conditions such as eczema.

Rich Roasted Garlic Dressing

What could be better in dressing than roasted garlic? Nothing! It's got rich flavor, sweetness, and creamy texture to perk up your bowl of salad. It looks like a "naughty" dressing, but it has so many health benefits. This could become one of your favorites.

6 full bulbs garlic
⅓ cup (75 mL) extra virgin olive oil
⅓ cup (75 mL) apple cider or white
   wine vinegar
1 tsp (5 mL) balsamic vinegar or soy sauce
salt and pepper to taste
½ tsp (2 mL) dried parsley
½ tsp (2 mL) dried oregano or basil
additional water for thinning if necessary

To roast garlic, simply cut off the top part of the garlic bulb. Set the cut bulbs into a baking pan with about ½ inch (1 cm) of water, with the cut side (that exposes the cloves) down. Bake at 375°F (190°C) for 45 minutes to an hour, replacing a bit of the water if it all evaporates.

When the cloves are all softened, remove them from the pan and set them aside. When they're cool enough to touch, squeeze the entire bulb of garlic from the bottom until the cloves pop out. Lightly mash them with a fork and sprinkle the roasted garlic with salt, pepper, and herbs if desired, or eat as is.

Take all the ingredients and combine them in a bowl. Whisk them well and pour over salad immediately. Enjoy.

For those who find a lot of garlic too harsh (imagine!), roasted garlic might be better. It's more mellow and has a sweetness to it.

Roasted garlic can be used as a spread on breads and crackers. Use it on pizzas, salads or in any dish where you need something a little different. A lot of people whip it into mashed potatoes.

Try drizzling your best extra virgin olive oil and balsamic vinegar on a beautiful plate and plunk a whole bulb of roasted garlic (free of its skin) in the middle. Serve with breadsticks or tiny breads. Wow!

Here's a big hit for a barbecue party. Use the same method, just wrap the garlic bulbs in foil, add a bit of water and cook on medium heat on the grill. A thinly sliced baguette is perfect for spreading the garlic on.

I think things should be easy to eat, so I don't usually get architectural. You know that thing male chefs do where everything has to be piled up, say, 10 inches high? (I wonder what Freud would have said about that.) But, appetizers are the exception; I think they can be a bit more "out there."

The idea with appetizers is to create something inviting and enticing. Appetizers set the mood for what's to come. So, think about what kind of atmosphere you want to create. There's light-hearted and whimsical, mysterious and earthy, dynamic and urban, rustic and homey or something sophisto, youthful, retro. YOU get to evoke the feelings and bask in the mood you've whipped up. Never think of it as pressure. Your family and friends will have a great time if you have a great time. Even if you're by yourself, you deserve fancy plates as much as a crowd.

There's something charming about the smaller version of things. Finger food is automatic fun. Also there's something unique and individualistic about everyone getting his or her own small plate, with something exciting to preview the meal.

This is a great way to turn people (including kids) on to new flavors; they seem more open-minded when it's not the actual meal.

Appetizers rev us up for the meal ahead. So think about delicious flavors that will create anticipation for what's next. Whether it's an elaborate antipasto platter, or a few cut up veggies and dip, amazing flavors will take you in the direction you want to go.

Beautiful, healthy, rejuvenating foods excite and inspire us. Appetizers immediately make an occasion feel special. Simple appetizers, presented well, are gorgeous. Splurge! It doesn't have to be expensive. Just indulge yourself and the people around you.

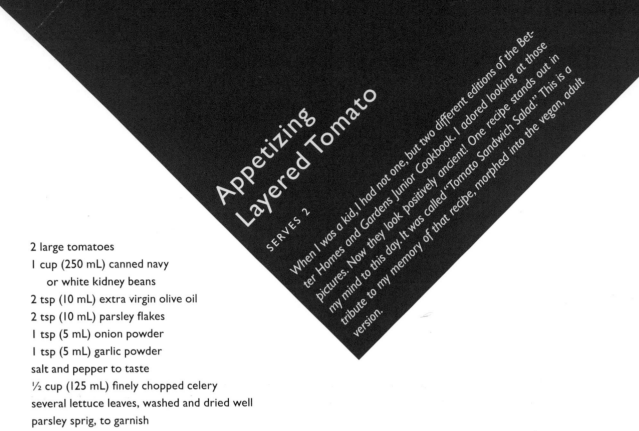

Appetizing Layered Tomato

SERVES 2

When I was a kid, I had not one, but two different editions of the Better Homes and Gardens Junior Cookbook. I adored looking at those pictures. Now they look positively ancient! One recipe stands out in my mind to this day. It was called "Tomato Sandwich Salad." This is a tribute to my memory of that recipe, morphed into the vegan, adult version.

2 large tomatoes
1 cup (250 mL) canned navy
   or white kidney beans
2 tsp (10 mL) extra virgin olive oil
2 tsp (10 mL) parsley flakes
1 tsp (5 mL) onion powder
1 tsp (5 mL) garlic powder
salt and pepper to taste
½ cup (125 mL) finely chopped celery
several lettuce leaves, washed and dried well
parsley sprig, to garnish

Slice the tomatoes across so that when they sit upright there are three rings with the cuts going horizontal. Set them aside. Then mash or process the navy beans so they're smooth and add the olive oil, parsley, onion and garlic powders, salt and pepper, celery and stir well.

Place the lettuce leaves on a plate (one plate per tomato/person) and place the first tomato ring (bottom of the tomato) on top of the lettuce. Spread generously with the bean mixture, and then add the next tomato ring, more bean mixture, last tomato top, and the parsley sprig on top. Repeat for the other tomato.

Serve with a great Dijon mustard or your favorite salad dressing on the side. This is also perfect for a nice light lunch, with some watercress or arugula finger sandwiches.

Party, party! This is a really fun appetizer for a dinner party. If you want to present it really nicely, put it on one end of a long, flat plate. The other side can have a drizzle of dressing, with a gremolata of nuts, seeds and a few bits of chopped veggies and some lemon slices—gorgeous!

Guac Boats

SERVES 2

Guacamole is fantastic. This decadent, green dip is positively addictive. If possible, try to keep some avocados handy. "Mole" (pronounced like olé) simply means a sauce of Mexican origin.

2 ripe avocados
2 cloves garlic, finely minced
½ tsp (2 mL) onion powder
squirt of fresh lemon or lime juice
salt and pepper to taste

First make the guacamole. Take a gorgeous, ripe avocado, cut it carefully in half and remove the pit. Remove most of the lovely green insides, leaving enough for the skin to have some strength. Repeat this with the other avocado. In a separate bowl, lightly mash the avocados with the garlic and onion powders. Squirt lemon or lime juice over the top, season it with salt and pepper to taste, and then give it another brief stir.

To assemble, put two skins from one avocado on each plate. Refill the skins with equal amounts of "guac." You could also add some salsa to each, one hot, one not. Or you could add all of the guac to one of the "boats" and the other one could just be filled with salsa. Use something funky to stick out of the top of each, like little stalks of celery with leaves, umbrellas, little flags, etc. This is perfect for serving with tortilla chips or thin crackers. Or you could fill one boat with the guac and the other with the chips.

You could do the exact same thing with the guacamole, then add shredded lettuce and chopped tomato to the top and serve as individual salads for a romantic dinner.

This is another great recipe to let kids make. Have everything cut in advance and let them go to it.

The lemon in this gives it that special zap. You can also use light vinegar, which is a nice change of pace.

Another version of this would be to put a lot of finely chopped celery and green or red pepper mixed in with the guac. It's a crunchier experience.

In the Philippines, avocado puréed with sugar and milk is a popular dessert drink.

Baby Spinach Burgers

SERVES 2 FOR LUNCH, 4 FOR A SNACK

I've never understood the bad press about spinach. Those who hate it must have had it canned or overcooked and it turned them off forever. Some people who won't eat spinach in any other form like this dish. Spinach really is one of the most divine creations of the planet.

10-oz (275-g) package frozen spinach
½ cup (125 mL) good breadcrumbs
½ cup (125 mL) fine cornmeal
1 medium sweet onion, finely chopped
3 cloves garlic, finely minced
1 tsp (5 mL) Italian seasoning
1 tsp (5 mL) sage
salt and pepper to taste
1 tsp (5 mL) soy sauce
1 Tbsp (15 mL) Dijon mustard
2 tsp (10 mL) nutritional yeast
1 Tbsp (15 mL) olive oil
pinch red pepper flakes (optional)

Preheat oven to 400°F (200°C)

Thaw the spinach and drain it well. Squeeze the water out so it's practically dry. Mix it together with the other ingredients. Squeeze a bit of the mixture in your fist to see if it sticks together well. If it's not there yet, add a little more oil or mustard.

Form little patties, about 2 inches (5 cm) across and place on a lightly olive oiled baking sheet or on one lined with parchment. Bake in the oven at about 400°F (200°C), for about 15 minutes, or until the edges are crispy and the patties are a nice golden brown color. Serve them plain or try them with a dip. These can be addictive if you like spinach, and maybe even if you don't!

Spinach is a good source of iron, Vitamins A and C, minerals and fiber and it contains some protein. It's a great way to liven up a plate (and you).

Frozen spinach is truly great when you're in a hurry and it's very cost-effective. It's great in anything baked, for dips and anything you just want to stir a little green into.

You could do these little patties with anything fresh and green if you don't want to use spinach. If you can get a lot of flat-leaf parsley, some arugula, mustard or collard greens, or lots of fresh herbs, that would be terrific.

Baby Spinach Burgers

Fruit Cup Breezer

SERVES 4

This is an old recipe that makes me think of childhood holidays. It's a paradox of a recipe—light, yet heavy, simple but exotic. You could make this any time of year to make any occasion special. I've always had this as an appetizer, but it would make an equally good dessert.

3 bananas cut into rounds
    or smaller
3 oranges, peeled, separated
    and cut into ½ segments
3 pears, cut into small pieces
3 apples, cut into small pieces
grapes, about 30 or so, cut in half
½ cup (125 mL) walnuts, chopped
1 cup (250 mL) good sherry or cherry liqueur
sprigs of mint, to garnish

Put all the ingredients into a bowl and pour the sherry or liqueur over the top. Stir gently and well and let it sit a couple of minutes for flavors to meld, but certainly not long enough to let the bananas darken. Spoon it into individual serving bowls and top with mint sprigs, to garnish.

When I was a kid, this was often made with a liqueur called Cherry Kiafa, which was super popular at the time. I like to use Kirsch. It's a clear, dry brandy made in the Black Forest of Germany from the fermented juice of the black morello cherry. Amaretto or Frangelico would be good too, to bring out the nutty character of this dish.

Fruit salads are a great way to incorporate several fruits into your day. Try different combinations. Adults and kids alike love 'em.

If you have a big fruit salad for lunch at work (instead of fast or fatty food) you won't believe the difference in your energy level.

Drunken Mushrooms

These are so simple, yet so amazing. I prepared "Drunken, Nutty Mushrooms" on a show once, where the boozy mushrooms were coated with crushed nuts, then barbecued. They're great and you can certainly do that if you like. This, however, is a quick version that has a charm all its own. Try some as soon as you can.

about 48 crimini mushrooms

4 red onions, cut into about 1½ inch
    (4 cm) pieces

2 green peppers, cut into about 1 inch
    (2.5 cm) pieces

2 red peppers, cut the same

1 cup (250 mL) rye (or other whiskey)

½ cup dark red wine (Burgundy would be good)

¾ cup (175 mL) olive oil

½ cup (125 mL) dark mushroom soy sauce

8 cloves garlic

2 tsp (10 mL) oregano

salt and pepper to taste

Preheat the oven to 425°F (220°C) or preheat the barbecue.

Put the mushrooms, onions and peppers into a large, flat pan with sides (like a lasagna pan). Blend all the remaining ingredients with an upright or hand blender to make a marinade. Pour over the veggies, cover, and marinate for at least half an hour. Pierce onto skewers.

Don't toss out the marinade! Put it in a pan and reduce over low heat for a gorgeous rye and mushroom nectar to drizzle on those mushrooms.

Barbecue the skewers on medium heat, turning frequently. Or bake in a 425°F (220°C) oven for 20 minutes, turning once. They need to only be cooked through, but some people like them cooked well, so experiment and have fun!

Most people don't realize how risky it is to pick wild mushrooms. Even if you've been picking in the same patch your whole life, they can change chemical content; people have died from eating them doing exactly that. So unless you enjoy playing Russian Roulette, go for the commercial kind.

If you like the sound of these flavors, but don't feel like skewering, put it all in a baking dish and throw it in the oven. Or use foil and do it on the barbecue.

A perfect dinner would be these mushrooms, a gorgeous herby rice pilaf, some barbecued corn on the cob and a salad. Heaven.

Bulgar-Stuffed Avocados

SERVES 2

This is a great starter for a summer dinner party. It makes outdoor dining special, so have all the components ready in advance. Then all you'll have to do is open the avocado and assemble the dish. That way you won't miss time with people when everything's in full swing.

1 cup (250 mL) bulgar wheat
2 ripe avocados
1 red onion, finely diced
2 tomatoes, finely diced
¼ cup (60 mL) cilantro, finely chopped
drizzle of extra virgin olive oil
drizzle of lemon or lime juice
salt and pepper to taste

Soak the bulgar wheat in hot water to cover it, plus a little extra, for about 20 minutes. The bulgar wheat will expand. Drain off all the water.

Cut the avocados in half and remove the pits. Carefully remove the green insides and set them aside. Combine the bulgar, onion, tomatoes and cilantro in a bowl. Pour on a good, generous drizzle of olive oil and lemon juice and then season with salt and pepper.

Refill avocado skins with the mixture. Then slice the avocado and put it on top. Add a sprinkle of salt to the avocados, garnish them with cilantro if you desire and serve immediately.

This dish is fresh, fun and filling enough to tide you over for a while. It also works well as one of the components of an all-appetizers supper.

This would be great served with some freshly warmed tortilla chips and Unexpected Dip (page 148) or a huge bowl of homemade salsa.

In Brazil, avocados are sometimes added to ice cream!

60% of all the avocados in California are grown in San Diego County.

Even though avocados have that rich, buttery consistency, they contain no cholesterol.

Bulgar wheat and avocados are a naturally good combination. Add some avocado when you make tabbouleh for an added sensation.

Bulgar-Stuffed Avocados

In my rather bohemian home, where we rarely adhere to schedules or the constraints of society, one of the few constants is pasta night. Every Sunday, I throw on a huge pot of garlic, onions and other vegetables to simmer for hours. At some point I add the tomatoes or sauce and the house smells wickedly good. Everyone looks forward to that night.

You can tell me the dangers of carbs till you're blue in the face—I'm not giving up pasta. Perish the thought. I'll eat more whole wheat pastas or eat less of them. I'll replace it with grains in their whole form sometimes. But give it up, *never*.

Refined carbs turn to sugars quickly and jet right into the bloodstream. If you're a diabetic it's best to avoid them altogether. You could instead eat whole grains with these sauces. For everyone else, limit your servings, hard as that may be. If you add lots of gorgeous mushrooms and chunks of fresh seasonal vegetables to your sauce, there'll be plenty on the plate to keep you busy. Or double up on a big Italian style salad first.

Always cook your pasta al dente which means "to the tooth" in Italian. I'm obsessive about this: pasta with no bite is totally pointless. To achieve al dente pasta, simply follow the package instructions. If the pasta is fresh, cooking takes less time, sometimes only a couple of minutes. You'll want to add your pasta to water that's at a full, rolling boil.

To drain pasta, simply strain it; there's no need to rinse. You'll need those starches on the pasta to hold the sauce. If you aren't adding the sauce immediately, drizzle the pasta with extra virgin olive oil and give it a light toss so it doesn't stick together. I hope you use some of these pasta night ideas and come up with new ones for your own fabulous sauces. Have fun.

PASTA PERFECTION

The Ultimate Deluxe Supreme Pasta Sauce

SERVES A CROWD

This sauce is for those special times when you want to cook and hang out in the kitchen. It's not complex, it's just that there are lots of ingredients and it's really best if it cooks all day. There are endless debates on the subject, but I think you should simmer sauce for as long as you can. Pour a big, honkin' glass of red wine and do something fun while it cooks.

½ cup (125 mL) onion, finely chopped

4 cloves garlic, finely chopped

1 stalk celery, finely chopped

½ cup (125 mL) zucchini, finely diced

2 Tbsp (30 mL) olive oil or vegetable broth to cover

4 ripe tomatoes, peeled and seeded OR 3 cups (750 mL) tomato sauce

1 green pepper, cut as you wish

1 red pepper, cut as you wish

½ carrot, grated

1 cup (250 mL) mushrooms, (Crimini or Portobello), sliced

1 cup (250 mL) parsley, finely chopped

2 green onions, finely chopped

½ cup (125 mL) cooked or canned lentils or softened bulgar wheat OR 11-oz (312-g) package of vegetarian ground "beef"

1 tsp (5 mL) capers

½ cup (125 mL) basil, finely chopped

½ cup (125 mL) olives, pitted and halved (kalamata are great)

½ cup (125 mL) artichokes, halved

salt to taste, if desired

½ tsp (2 mL) black pepper

1 tsp (5 mL) oregano

red pepper flakes, if desired

water as needed to reduce thicknesss

½ cup (125 mL) red wine, if desired

Add the onions, garlic, celery and zucchini in a good-sized pot. Add the olive oil or cover with broth. Turn the heat to medium and watch that it doesn't stick, stirring often. At this point, if you have fresh tomatoes, you can chop them finely and add them. When the onions are translucent and everything is soft enough to process, blend the whole thing in a food processor, blender or with a hand blender.

Add the peppers, carrot, mushrooms, parsley, green onions, the lentils (or bulgar or vegetarian ground "beef") and the tomato sauce. Put the sauce on medium until it comes to a boil and then reduce the heat to low, to maintain a simmer. Add some water or broth as well, unless there's still a lot of liquid.

Let it slow cook for as long as you possibly can: the longer, the better, the thicker and richer. If you're going to have it on for hours, remember to keep checking the liquid and stirring regularly. There are a lot of ingredients here so keep an eye on it—not constantly, just give it a stir and check your liquid every 15–20 minutes.

When dinner's in sight, and the sauce has reached the desired thickness, add the capers, basil, olives, artichokes, salt and pepper, oregano, red pepper flakes and wine if desired. Let simmer for another half an hour or so on the lowest heat to let the flavors merge.

This one's not wimpy so it will stand up to any pasta you love. You can even forget about making a salad, this thing is a meal unto itself. I hope you get to eat this with people you love, and wallow in the praise you'll get. It's the Mother of All Sauces.

This sauce freezes perfectly, so make a huge pot and divide it into useable serving sizes, then freeze it. When you're in a rush, throw that in a pot and reconstitute it. Your kitchen will fill with the intoxicating aroma and dinner will be done in a flash.

This is a perfect sauce to make in a slow cooker. Make ahead, boil up your pasta at the last minute and enjoy.

Miso-Soaked Whole Wheat Spirals

SERVES 4

This was originally a mistake. I use a gas stove with a cast iron top, so because of the heat of the pilot light, some of the burners are always quite hot, even when they're turned off. One day, I had some miso broth, with pasta in it and didn't get back to it for about an hour. This delightful surprise was what I discovered.

2 heaping Tbsp (30 mL) light miso
2 cups (500 mL) whole wheat rotini
½ cup (125 mL) carrots, cut into
    matchsticks
½ cup (125 mL) green onion, finely chopped
½ cup (125 mL) parsley
drizzle olive oil

Bring about 4 cups (1 L) of water to a boil and add the miso. When it's boiling, add the pasta and the other ingredients. As soon as the pasta's al dente, turn the heat down as low as it'll go (almost off). Leave it until almost all of the water has evaporated or has been absorbed into the pasta. Remove from the heat and drizzle it with olive oil. Add the carrots, green onion and parsley, then serve.

Hope you love it.

This is strong on the miso—the way I like it. You can certainly reduce the amount if you find it too harsh. (This also depends, of course, on the particular type of miso you're using).

This would be great with some steamed collard greens or a spinach salad, with a tangy dressing on the side. It definitely screams for a snap of green.

You could also prepare your pasta like this and then drizzle it with the olive oil, stir it and cool it in the fridge. Then add some fresh chopped veggies for an intensely miso-y pasta salad.

You could sprinkle this with sesame seeds and a bit of paprika for color. If you don't think it's flavorful enough (I can't imagine this happening, but I like to project for even the strangest of events!) consider a drizzle of soy or tamari (Japanese wheat-free soy sauce).

Millionaire Sauce

This is for when you're feeling rich. Hey, it's cheaper than diamonds. Look out—this sauce may become addictive to even those who can't afford it. It's rich and it's absolutely wonderful. This turns a platter of ziti into a masterpiece. Use only the finest organic produce and be sinfully selective.

1 Tbsp (15 mL) of your finest extra virgin olive oil

4 cloves garlic, finely chopped

4 shallots, finely chopped

10 perfect vine-ripened tomatoes, peeled, seeded and chopped

1 cup (250 mL) of the best red wine you can afford

½ cup (125 mL) sun-dried tomatoes, softened and chopped finely

1 cup (250 mL) tomato sauce

6 Portobello mushrooms, whole

a couple of truffles†, finely sliced

1 cup (250 mL) morel mushrooms, sliced

½ cup (125 mL) fresh basil, chopped

1 bunch of fresh asparagus tips, steamed, cut in half

2 tsp (10 mL) truffle oil †

1 Tbsp (15 mL) capers

½ cup (125 mL) toasted pecans, crushed

2 tsp (10 mL) saffron

best French sea salt you can get, to taste (Fleur de Sel is great)

Heat the garlic and shallots in the olive oil in a good-sized pan. Turn the heat to medium, stirring constantly and then cook them until the shallots are translucent. Add the tomatoes and cook for a few minutes, stirring constantly. Add the wine, the sun-dried tomatoes and the tomato sauce. Turn the heat down to medium-low and allow it to simmer for 10 minutes or so to incorporate the flavors.

Add the mushrooms. It's nice if each person gets a whole one on his or her plate. If you want to slice them, go ahead, they'll still carry tons of impact. Next, add the truffles and the morels. The morels are a lot smaller; cut them if you want to but it's not necessary. Cover and turn the heat down to low. Simmer for at least an hour.

Shortly before serving, add the basil, asparagus, truffle oil, capers, pecans and the saffron. Then serve over the most fabulous pasta you can find. Some fresh fettuccine would be perfect. Or some large pecan or spinach-stuffed ravioli would work beautifully. This sauce would also be yummy with risotto, over any plate of whole grains or serve over a heaping mound of hearty greens like freshly blanched escarole.

† Truffles and truffle oil are available in specialty or gourmet markets.

Because truffles are grown underground and are hard to get at, they're killer expensive. Black truffles can be more than $500 a pound—ouch.

Morel mushrooms have an intensely earthy flavor and are highly-prized. Since they're now grown commercially, you can usually find dried ones in the supermarket. Try them in sauces, stuffings and grain dishes.

Lazy Pasta Sauce

SERVES 4–6

As much as I want that luxurious Sunday night supper, sometimes we get home too late and it's a school night. For the ease of this recipe though, it tastes pretty fabulous. Once again proving that food-wise, simplicity is okay.

1 Tbsp (15 mL) olive oil

½ cup (125 mL) onion, finely diced
   or thinly sliced

3 cloves garlic, finely chopped

½ cup (125 mL) water (or other liquid)

4 cups (1 L) tomato sauce

½ cup (125 mL) fresh parsley, finely chopped

salt and pepper to taste

½ cup (125 mL) red wine, optional

½ tsp (2 mL) each of basil and/or oregano,
   red pepper flakes to taste

Put the olive oil, onion and garlic into a hot pan and stir constantly on high, until the onions are translucent. Add the water if they start to stick or aren't cooked down yet. You can skip the oil and use only water if you want it to be a non-fat sauce. Turn the heat down to medium-low, add the tomato sauce and parsley and then cover and simmer it for as long as you have time to. As the sauce thickens, you'll have to watch it carefully and perhaps add more water. Turn it down to low for simmering. Taste and add seasoning and additions as desired.

The longer this sauce cooks, the more delectable it will be. You could add any other vegetables you like such as peppers, mushrooms, zucchini—really anything you've got on hand. Chop it finely so it will cook faster.

Pasta is a good alternative for when you're in a hurry. Instead of having an elaborate Sunday pasta night, you could just reserve it for when you're in a panic!

When you bring home the groceries, cut and chop those veggies. You could then store the components of a bunch of different sauces in freezer bags. That's such a time saver later in the week.

This sauce is excellent the next day and freezes perfectly, so consider doubling the recipe. Or give half to a friend. You're doing the work anyway for one batch and it means so much to get anything home-made in this microwave world.

Giant Ravioli Stuffed with Walnuts and Cashews

Giant Ravioli Stuffed with Walnuts and Cashews

SERVES 6

This dish shows that you don't have to try and replicate actual meat, but it's nice to have something "meaty" now and again. No one would argue that a nut is the same as a steak, but this works as a replacement for the meaty component in so many meals. While making the pasta, keep in mind that various flours absorb liquid differently. I encourage you to experiment with different kinds of flours.

RAVIOLI

3 cups (750 mL) whole wheat flour

1 cup (250 mL) water

½ tsp (2 mL) salt

2 cups (500 mL) Nutmeat (see recipe below)

WALNUT & CASHEW NUTMEAT

1 Tbsp (15 mL) olive oil

1 large onion, finely chopped

1 whole bulb garlic, finely chopped

3 cups (750 mL) mushrooms, sliced then chopped

3 cups (750 mL) spinach leaves, coarsely chopped
(or frozen, thawed and well-drained)

1 cup (250 mL) walnuts, coarsely chopped

1 cup (250 mL) cashews, coarsely chopped

2 Tbsp (30 mL) dark mushroom soy sauce

salt and pepper to taste

additional seasonings such as oregano, basil, sage, ground
cumin (optional)

FOR THE RAVIOLI

Combine the ravioli ingredients in a bowl, using two cups of the flour. Keeping your hands well-floured, knead the dough lightly. Continue to knead and add flour until it has enough body to hold up. It should have some elasticity and not be too sticky. Wrap in plastic wrap and chill until needed.

Cooking instructions continued on following page . . .

Add the olive oil to a hot pan and sauté the onions and garlic until the onions are translucent. Add the mushrooms and sauté. Remove the pan from the heat, stir in the spinach and set aside.

In a completely dry pan, toast the walnuts on medium-high heat for 1 or 2 minutes or until aromatic, shaking the pan constantly. Set the walnuts aside, add the cashews to the hot pan and cover them with water. Cook uncovered on medium heat until the water evaporates. Remove from the heat and combine with the onion/mushroom mixture.

Add the dark soy sauce, combine well, then taste. Add salt, pepper and any additional seasonings if desired.

TO ASSEMBLE

When making any kind of pasta, nothing can go too far astray, so don't worry. The only thing with ravioli is keeping in the filling. And if it falls out it's not the end of the world. It's only ravioli.

Roll about ¼ of the dough at a time on a floured board, adding flour as needed. Although some pastas are meant to be paper-thin—with ravioli that isn't necessary. If it doesn't fall apart when you try to lift it, you're ready. Cut it into 6-inch (15-cm) strips. Spoon the nutmeat on one side of the strip, about 1½ inches (4 cm) across. Do this every 2 inches (5 cm) or so. Lightly lift the edge of what will be each ravioli.

Have a bowl of water ready. Use your fingers to "paint" the water where the ravioli will connect—it's your glue. Then, carefully fold them over and gently press the dough down, attempting to do so from the middle out, so that the air will escape (this makes them less likely to break). Cut the ravioli with a sharp knife or a pizza cutter and seal the edges with the tines of a fork or your fingers. Set them on a well-floured surface or a floured piece of parchment.

Bring a large pot of water to a boil and add the ravioli—they're done when they float to the top. Remove, strain them and gently place them in the sauce of your choice.

Use the Nutmeat to top or mix with pasta or rice, to stuff ravioli, to stuff vegetables, to add to stir-fried vegetables, sauces, chilis, stews, to roll up in wraps, fill perogies, samosas and a million other brilliant uses you'll no doubt come up with.

Three or four of these ravioli on a plate, covered in sauce, make a great main course. Or have one or two as a starter or side dish. You can certainly use whatever filling you desire. Plain cooked spinach and onion is fantastic, or mushroom has a wonderful meaty quality that works well with this recipe. You can also make the ravioli plate-sized, which people freak with happiness over. You can use large fillings like Portobello mushroom slices, ½ flattened roasted red pepper, etc. There's something wild about getting a giant ravioli on your plate.

Although this particular nut combination is unreal, don't hesitate to try it with pecans, almonds, hazelnuts or any other kind you might have on hand.

Pasta Bows with Capers and Onions

SERVES 4–6

This easy pasta dish is fun to prepare and fun to eat. It's a bit different and makes a great side dish or a main course. It's equally delicious served hot or cold.

4 cups pasta bows
¼ cup (60 mL) olive oil
1 clove garlic, finely minced
1 fresh tomato, skinned, seeded and finely diced
1 Tbsp (15 mL) fresh parsley, finely minced
¼ cup (60 mL) capers
½ red onion, sliced as finely as possible
a few fresh basil leaves, chopped
1 tsp (5 mL) fresh lemon juice
salt and pepper to taste

Boil the water and cook the pasta al dente. Drizzle it with olive oil, stir and set it aside, covered.

Drizzle a pan with olive oil. Heat it up to medium and put in the garlic, tomato, parsley, capers and the paper-thin onion. Cook it just long enough to heat it and bring out the bright green of the parsley. Put it over the pasta, along with the basil, lemon juice and salt and pepper if you desire.

Serve and enjoy.

Fresh, cold red peppers stuffed with a variety of cool seasonal vegetables would be fantastic with this dish.

Capers are tiny green buds that are dried in the sun and pickled in vinegar. There are delicate ones from France or large, caper berries with stems (the size of olives) from Spain. They add a pungent note to many dishes.

Rowdy Red Pepper Sauce

SERVES 4–6

I only make this when I can get a huge amount of red peppers for a reasonable price (once a year!) but perhaps you're into canning and can enjoy this more often. You don't need the tomato—there's a certain charm when this red, red sauce doesn't have any. I love the way the peppers taste with a hint of tomato though. So try it with just the peppers first and if you want to add the sauce, go for it.

5 gorgeous red peppers
5 cloves garlic, peeled
water or vegetable stock for cooking down
salt and pepper to taste
1 tsp (5 mL) oregano
1 tsp (5 mL) basil
½ cup (125 mL) tomato sauce (optional)
½ cup (125 mL) fresh basil, finely chopped, if available

Cut the peppers in half, wash and remove the seeds and white pith. Place the peppers into a big pot with at least 6 inches (15 cm) of water at the bottom, cover and bring to a boil. Reduce the heat to medium and stir occasionally. When the skins start peeling off, remove and drain the peppers. Immerse them in a bowl of cold water.

I never peel them; I think the skins taste fine and I just purée them up with the rest of the sauce. So I'll leave it up to you. If you're removing the skins, do so, then return the peppers to the hot water pot and continue to cook them. Add the garlic (whole cloves are fine) and all other ingredients except for the tomato sauce and basil. Cover them and continue to cook them on medium-low for another hour, checking periodically to make sure there's enough water so it doesn't stick. Just add water a bit at a time when the peppers get really tender because you don't want it to be too watery.

When the ingredients are very tender, blend everything with an upright or hand blender until it's as smooth as you can get it. Check the seasonings and adjust accordingly. If desired, add the tomato sauce, heat up again and stir well to meld flavors.

Fresh basil is the perfect addition to this. If you have any, chop it coarsely and just add to the top of the sauce on each plate when serving.

This sauce is fantastic with polenta or other things made from cornmeal. You could break open a freshly baked corn muffin, pour a ladle of this sauce overtop and finish with black beans and green onions. Try it as a dip too.

Naturally colored food is good for you (think beta carotene, which is good for boosting your immune system).

Macaroni and "Cheese"

SERVES 2

This recipe is about mimicking the color of cheese, and creating a suggestion of the taste. The nutritional yeast has a fermented quality that implies cheese, while the soy milk provides the protein-rich component. The oil gives the decadence. You can add any cooked vegetables you wish to make this even better. Lots of finely chopped green onions, stirred in just before baking, are delicious.

3 Tbsp (45 mL) olive oil

3 cloves garlic, chopped

1 onion, chopped

¼ cup (60 mL) cooked carrot, cooked red pepper (or both)

2 cups (500 mL) cooked macaroni (whole wheat elbows)

2 heaping Tbsp (30 mL) nutritional yeast

1 Tbsp (15 mL) parsley, finely chopped

about ½ cup (125 mL) unsweetened soy milk

½ tsp (2 mL) turmeric

1 tsp (5 mL) paprika (plus a pinch for the top)

salt and pepper to taste

½ cup (125 mL) good breadcrumbs (optional)

Preheat oven to 350°F (180°C).

In about 1 Tbsp (15 mL) of olive oil, cook the garlic and onion on medium, stirring, until they're translucent. Then take the onion and garlic, and the carrot or red pepper and blend them with a hand or upright blender until smooth, adding a bit of soy milk if necessary.

Combine all the other ingredients, except the breadcrumbs. Put the macaroni into an olive oiled 9-inch (23-cm) pie plate or other baking pan. Sprinkle the breadcrumbs on top if you're using them, with a pinch of paprika for color. Bake at 350°F (180°C) for about 25 minutes, or until golden brown.

Another way you could do this is to make a roux with the onion and garlic and 1 Tbsp (15 mL) of flour. Then, mix in the soy milk, whisking constantly and just blend with this thicker version of sauce when you combine the ingredients. Or purée a ½ cup (125 mL) of navy beans into this as the thickening agent—that works well too.

The lactose-free cheese replacement products you find in the stores usually still contain casein. That's the protein part of the milk. However, recently I have discovered a brand that does not contain casein—so read those labels. It's delicious, but it doesn't melt, so although you could grate it and add it to something like this, I probably wouldn't.

A tasty addition to this dish is slivered almonds, if you like a bit of crunch.

Another way to serve regular or vegan mac-n-cheese is to put some salsa on the side. You can add a forkful as you wish for some heat or tang.

This is the item—the one that strikes fear into people's hearts and sends them screaming into the night. Even though I love it now, I remember the first time I tried it just diced on a salad (recommended by some vegan cookbook)—gag me.

If you don't want to eat it, I promise I'll never try to convince you. I don't believe in sneaking it into people's food or saying it's the only way to get certain vitamins (there are other ways). I use it strictly because I like it. It's super-versatile and I can use it to create many meals I couldn't make otherwise.

There are all kinds of scary instructions in various cookbooks, which tell you that you have to "press it" (under heavy objects) to remove the liquid, etc. It's all a lot of nonsense. Years ago when you had to buy tofu from a briny vat in some hippie health food store, maybe tofu had to be pressed. But I've never pressed it and it always comes out fine. It's not a mystery how to cook it (or I'll make sure it isn't once I'm done with you—ha ha!).

It has some wonderful aspects I think you'll appreciate. For example, it takes on the flavors of other things beautifully, so it gets one of my "magical food" labels. It can be made into balls, whipped, cut into sticks, made into loaves, cut into little cubes, transformed into quiches, mousses, shakes and something that resembles eggs. It's a great thing to have in the kitchen.

The recipes I've included here will give you a good jumping-off point for using tofu. Tofu requires a little extra seasoning, but it's worth the effort. I promise it won't ever be bland, and I'll NEVER recommend you just dice it and throw it on a salad. Yucccckkkkk.

TERRIFYING TOFU

Tofu Stuffed Tomatoes

SERVES 4

This is a yummy recipe if you're used to tofu and nutritional yeast. It's not something I'd try on someone who's leery of those items. It has a lot of flavor, but the texture is mostly soft (the green onions give it a bit of crunch). You could always sprinkle on some nuts, seeds or finely chopped celery for added bite if you like.

I love these tomatoes as a summer lunch, served on a generous bed of spinach with Faux Caesar Dressing (page 56) on the side. Try them when you're in the mood for something different.

2 Tbsp (30 mL) olive oil

2 cups (500 mL) medium to firm tofu

2 Tbsp (30 mL) soy sauce

3 green onions, finely chopped

4 medium-large, ripe tomatoes

½ tsp (2 mL) garlic powder

½ tsp (2 mL) onion powder

½ tsp (2 mL) Italian seasoning (if desired)

salt and pepper to taste

3 Tbsp (45 mL) nutritional yeast

½ cup (125 mL) freshly chopped parsley or chopped
   organic greens

In a pan lightly coated with olive oil (or other liquid), heat up the tofu, adding soy sauce as you go. You can add the green onions and cook them, or add them at the end for more intensity. Add seasonings and heat it through, turning and adding a little soy sauce at a time. If it starts to stick, turn down the heat. It just has to heat enough to bring out the flavors. Add the nutritional yeast. Taste and adjust the seasonings if necessary. Remove from the heat and set aside.

You need good, firm tomatoes for this. Cut a little hat out of the top of the tomato, and scoop out the wet part in the middle. Use caution not to cut through the tomato. It's like scooping a pumpkin, only way more delicate. Fill each tomato to capacity and replace the little tomato hat on top for a lid.

You could heat these up, but they're awesome at room temperature. The raw tomato is firmer and more delicious.

Tofu is sometimes referred to as "bean curd." In Asian markets you can get a yellow, fibrous-looking flat substance also referred to as bean curd that can be wrapped around things for tasty and unusual dishes.

Buddhist missionaries, who were vegetarian, took tofu out of the Orient to share with India. Since it picks up flavors, it's brilliant with Indian cuisine.

Think about how only a precious few North Americans were into tofu in the '60s. Now most people have tried it in one form or another, at least in certain parts of the continent. You can get it in the grocery store—not only in specialty stores like a few years ago.

If you haven't tried black kale, it's amazing. It's firmer than a lot of leafy greens, so the cooking time isn't as picky. Its beautiful, rich color is a feast for the eye. And the taste and texture is perfect for a lot of dishes, including this one.

Heat a deep pan or sauté pan to medium-hot. Add the olive oil, onions, kale stalks, garlic and the carrot. Keep stirring until the onions are translucent, adding a little water if necessary. Add the tofu and kale leaves. Cover and turn the heat down to low. Cook for about 10 minutes and then add the tomato sauce, parsley, cumin and salt and pepper to taste. Cover, keep on low and cook for 10 minutes more. The sauce should be a light tomato sauce; if it's too thick add a little water and cook it on low till it's hot. Remove from the heat, add the teriyaki sauce and serve.

Serve this over rice, grains or pasta or just eat it from a deep bowl. Heaven! This is a good, savory meal for a cold day or when you need something to warm you up.

2 Tbsp (30 mL) olive oil

2 white onions, sliced

6 black kale stalks, finely chopped

5 cloves garlic, finely chopped

1 carrot, cut into rings

12 oz (350 g) block medium to firm tofu

6 large black kale leaves, cut into 4-inch (10-cm) pieces

2 cups (500 mL) tomato sauce

1 tsp (5 mL) parsley flakes

1 tsp (5 mL) ground cumin

1 Tbsp (15 mL) teriyaki sauce

If you've never had hot and sour soup, a fabulous Chinese creation, try some. It's a dish that some non-tofu types will accept, even though it contains tofu.

Kale is a member of the Brassica family, which also includes cabbage and Brussels sprouts. It's a super-nutritious food that has tons of anti-cancer potential.

A lightning-quick main course is to cut extra-firm tofu into strips, coat it completely in a super tangy barbecue sauce and pop it under the broiler till hot and bubbly.

Tofu "Fries"

These aren't fried at all and seem to be liked equally by kids and adults. They're a fun finger food that I usually use as a main course. They're also perfect for a snack or as party food.

two 12-oz (350-g) blocks firm
   or extra firm tofu (2 block package)
½ cup (125 mL) unsweetened soy milk
1 Tbsp (15 mL) olive oil
1 cup (250 mL) breadcrumbs or whole wheat flour
2 tsp (10 mL) garlic powder
2 tsp (10 mL) onion powder
1 Tbsp (15 mL) Italian seasoning
1 Tbsp (15 mL) parsley flakes
1 tsp (5 mL) paprika
salt and pepper to taste (generously)

Preheat oven to 400°F (200°C).

Cut the tofu into "fries." Just make slices and then cut them through about 4 times. Mix the soy milk and olive oil in a bowl. In another bowl, combine the other ingredients and mix well. Dip the tofu sticks into the soy milk and then press them into the breading mixture, coating each one fully. Place them on the lightly oiled baking sheet and bake for about 25 minutes. The "fries" should be slightly golden or firm to the touch. Serve with Bonanza Barbecue Sauce (page 165), ketchup or gravy.

Picnic Time—Wrap up these tofu fries and bring 'em on a picnic. They're still tasty at room temperature and so easy to pack.

The great thing about dishes like this is that you can season them any way and all are great. Try a Mexican version with cumin, chili powder, paprika and some cayenne pepper. Dip 'em in lime juice to make the coating stick.

You can cut the tofu into any shape you wish. If you have tiny cutters, go for some wild shapes—fun stuff for kids, or elegant for gourmet affairs.

In the first season of the TV show "Top Chef," chefs competed to win $100,000 and all kinds of accolades. On one episode, one of the chefs presented a dish that the judges considered too peppery. They kept referring to this fellow as "the pepper monkey." I loved the phrase and couldn't get it out of my head. Being a bit of a pepper monkey myself, I devised this dish to showcase that fact.

Preheat the oven to 350°F (180°C).

Oil a 13- x 9-inch (3.5-L) casserole dish with olive oil or cover the bottom with parchment. Slice the tofu into rectangles, about ½ inch (1 cm) thick. Set them into the pan, keeping each one flat if there's room. If not, layer them slightly. Mix the olive oil, balsamic, soy sauce, garlic and onion powders, ground cumin and sage. Saturate each piece of tofu in this mixture by pouring it over the top and turning each piece. Cover it with plastic wrap and let it sit for about 20 minutes for the tofu to absorb the flavor.

Uncover the tofu. Coat each tofu piece with a layer of freshly cracked pepper. Flip and repeat on the other side.

Pour the wine into the pan. Add all of the other ingredients, beginning with the onion.

Cover the peppery tofu with foil and pop it into the oven for half an hour. Then remove the foil and the vegetables. Put the broiler on high, but leave the pan in the middle of the oven. Cook on one side for about 4–5 minutes, then flip the tofu and cook the other side the same way.

Serve with a big salad. Some brown rice or sesame "fries" and miso gravy would be great. Make some soon, for your pepper monkey.

24-oz (700-g) 2 block package tofu
2 Tbsp (30 mL) olive oil
3 Tbsp (45 mL) balsamic vinegar
4 Tbsp (60 mL) dark soy sauce, or
    mushroom soy sauce
1 tsp (5 mL) garlic powder
1 tsp (5 mL) onion powder
½ tsp (2 mL) ground cumin
½ tsp (2 mL) sage
freshly cracked pepper
1 cup (250 mL) dry red wine
1 large onion, cut into quarters
1 carrot, coarsely chopped
1 cup (250 mL) parsley
2 cups (500 mL) crimini mushrooms,
    halved
1 red pepper, cut into rings
1 green pepper, cut into rings
a good sprinkling of coarse sea salt
drizzle of olive oil

To me, the perfect complement to this protein-laden dish would be a huge bed of fresh spinach with a light vinaigrette or Italian dressing on it. Just lay a couple of the peppered tofu slices and some of the vegetables on that and it'll look like a high-end restaurant meal.

Pepper, like salt, was so highly revered in ancient history that it became a form of currency.

A bunch of sautéed mushrooms always works with peppery things!

I understand that potatoes are one of those items that are thrown into the "fattening" pile because of the carb thing. The most weight I ever lost in my life was when I first became a vegetarian. My husband and I and our baby daughter were eating 20 lb of potatoes a week, but with no added fats. Now, I'm not saying you have to be that excessive, but when no fats are involved, it certainly allows you to eat more.

Although many of these recipes do contain oils, you don't have to add them if you want to cut out fats. Or just add a bit. There's always a way to put in something else that creates tremendous flavor, and there's always another cooking method.

For example, the typical way to eat a baked potato is to cover the damn thing in so much sour cream and chives that you can't even taste the potato. Did you ever try it with just the chives? Try a drizzle of olive oil, a splash of flavored vinegar, some pepper and salt and a ton of chives. To die for!

You can do so much with potatoes. They can be finely puréed, coarsely cut and crisped up under a broiler, or some form in-between. You can add one or two potatoes to enhance a one-pot meal. Potatoes taste great and absorb whatever flavors you combine them with.

Mashed white beans with a lot of garlic, or just roasted garlic, replace sour cream nicely. You can try salsa with a lot of added hot sauce, or some chopped roasted red peppers, a sprinkle of capers, some artichokes, etc. How about a spicy peanut sauce? Or any other Asian sauce or dressing without refined oils? Or just top it with chili. Mmmm, the possibilities are once again, endless.

POTATO OASIS

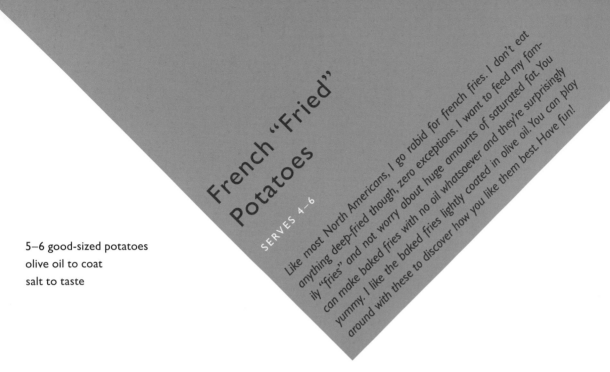

French "Fried" Potatoes

SERVES 4–6

Like most North Americans, I go rabid for french fries. I don't eat anything deep-fried though, zero exceptions. I want to feed my family "fries" and not worry about huge amounts of saturated fat. You can make baked fries with no oil whatsoever and they're surprisingly yummy. I like the baked fries lightly coated in olive oil. You can play around with these to discover how you like them best. Have fun!

5–6 good-sized potatoes
olive oil to coat
salt to taste

Preheat oven to 425°F (220°C).

Cut up the potatoes and put them into a large bowl. Drizzle them with olive oil, sprinkle with salt (or whatever seasoning you like) and toss well.

Now you could simply olive oil your baking sheet, or maybe you're into non-stick. I like to put down a piece of parchment paper. The potatoes won't stick and clean-up is so much easier.

You can bake these at about 425°F (220°C) and wait until they're done (seemingly forever) or do what I do and crank the oven up to 450°F (230°C) and just kind of keep an eye on them. If the oven is really hot, the outside ones will cook first, so you just give them a gentle flip now and again (burying the darker ones so they don't overcook). When they're good and golden, they're done.

Another good way to do this is to cover the potatoes with foil and bake them for half an hour so they can cook through first, before attempting to brown them at all. Then remove the foil and cook another 15 minutes, turning them a couple of times.

Do you like teeny-weeny shoestring potatoes or thickly cut wedgie home fries? I like something in-between, but it's an individual thing. So try some different cuts. Peel the potatoes, or if the peels are decent, you don't have to bother. If I'm able to buy nice organic ones that are reasonably clean, I'd never peel them because I like the peel.

Another great condiment for fries is a spicy horseradish mustard.

If you like ketchup with fries, for a nice twist, try them with salsa instead.

Spicy "Fries"

These are terrific if you feel like something special to have for a snack for a game night, or a really cool movie. They're fun, they're spicy, something to perk you up for that wild evening ahead, or even to get you through the middle of the workweek.

5–6 good-sized potatoes
olive oil to coat
salt and pepper to taste
½ tsp (2 mL) each of any or all of the following:
garlic powder, onion powder, ground cumin,
    sweet paprika, curry powder
cayenne pepper (optional)

Preheat oven to 425°F (220°C).

Follow the same basic French "Fried" Potatoes (page 88) recipe, and then add the extra flavorings, making them simply spicy or downright fiery!

TWO MORE VARIATIONS

Again, using the same French "Fried" Potatoes (page 88) recipe, try doing the same thing with sweet potatoes or yams. Both are a nice departure from the usual. The yams are sweet and delicious, but the sweet potatoes are like eating pure sugar, I kid you not. I seriously recommend that with kids you call them "candy" because they're so sweet that nobody will reject that concept! (Watch them more carefully than normal potatoes as the sugar content will make them more likely to burn.)

Coating potatoes with finely ground oatmeal that's highly seasoned, then baking, is another tempting treat.

For a sophisticated twist, put some dried mushrooms into the food processor and pulse them till they're powdery. Add any herbs and seasonings you wish and "dust" your potatoes before baking.

If you want to get really creative you can marinate potatoes before baking them. Try a vinaigrette for starters and work your way up to more intense marinades.

New Potatoes in Almond Cream

SERVES 4

This is a happily decadent recipe for when you're in the mood for something rich. It can stand alone or be a perfect complement to so many dishes. Add a few cooked wheat berries and some steamed broccoli florets for a wonderful main course.

15 new potatoes (the little
   seasonal ones), cooked, steamed
   or boiled until fork-tender
½ cup (125 mL) olive oil
½ cup (125 mL) onion, finely chopped or sliced
2 cloves garlic, finely minced
½ cup (125 mL) whole, blanched almonds
½ tsp (2 mL) onion powder
salt and pepper to taste
1 Tbsp (15 mL) light vinegar or lemon or lime juice
1 Tbsp (15 mL) fresh parsley, finely chopped
½ tsp (2 mL) Italian seasoning (basil, oregano,
   marjoram, etc.)
a few slivered almonds and fresh parsley sprigs, to garnish

Put the potatoes into a large bowl or a serving platter. If you wish to cut them in half or quarters, do so. Put the olive oil, onion, garlic, blanched almonds, onion powder, salt and pepper and vinegar or lemon juice together and blend it all with an upright or hand blender until smooth. If you require more liquid, add a bit more lemon, vinegar or olive oil, or equal parts of both. Adjust the seasonings accordingly.

Garnish with slivered almonds and parsley, if desired.

This dish is great with a lot of fresh, green stir-fried or steamed veggies that have a lot of flavor. It would be perfect with a whole bunch of beet greens dressed with something tangy.

This is a great dish to serve with some colorful vegetable kabobs on the side.

There are sweet almonds and bitter ones. The bitter are used to make almond oil that's used to flavor foods such as biscotti and cakes, and to flavor liqueurs like amaretto.

Potato Salad with a Twist

Here's a great no-mayo potato salad for picnics. It can sit around on a hot day with no worries about it going bad. You could add whatever else you like in this. Try a handful of toasted almonds, some olives, a bit of spinach, some grated carrot or whatever veggies you have on hand that you love. Nuts and seeds are good too. Add the orange or lime segments if you want more flavor. As always, you could add flavor some minced garlic. Take this basic recipe and jazz it up your way.

3 medium potatoes, boiled,
   then cubed, or cut into about
   2 inch (5 cm) pieces
¼ cup (60 mL) olive oil
3 green onions, cut into rings
1 cucumber, cut in half lengthwise, then sliced
   into half moons
1 stalk celery, finely chopped
½ cup (125 mL) flat-leaf parsley, finely chopped
½ cup (125 mL) cherry or grape tomatoes
¼ cup (60 mL) apple cider vinegar
1 Tbsp (15 mL) orange rind, grated
1 Tbsp (15 mL) lime rind, grated
2 Tbsp (30 mL) fresh orange juice
2 Tbsp (30 mL) fresh lime juice
salt and pepper to taste
½ cup (125 mL) fresh mint, finely chopped

Put the potatoes into a large bowl and then add the rest of the ingredients. Toss well, to incorporate the flavors. Cover and wait at least half an hour for the flavors to mingle.

The great thing about this is that the citrus juices also help to keep the potato from discoloring.

Try different varieties of potatoes in your salads. Recently I found the most adorable little red skinned organic potatoes that I baked, Greek style. They would have made the ultimate potato salad too.

Some people like a reasonable amount of greens in a potato salad, just as seasoning. Just for fun, try a ton of chopped arugula, cilantro, flat-leaf parsley, spinach or something delectably green and stir it in.

Crispy Potato Bombs

SERVES 4–6

I was watching a show about a restaurant (which was, I believe, owned by one or more of the band members of U2). They served this creation that was cooked potato put through a ricer, with some strips of ham, celeriac (yum!) and I think some carrots and onions or shallots. It was formed into balls and coated with panko (Japanese breadcrumbs). It was then deep-fried. I liked the idea, so I decided to make my own version.

2 Tbsp (30 mL) olive oil
   or cooking liquid (you could
   use the potato water)
1 large onion, chopped
6 cloves garlic, chopped
5 medium potatoes, boiled
5-oz (155-g) package vegetarian
   pepperoni, ham or the like
½ cup (125 mL) parsley, finely chopped
1 Tbsp Italian seasoning (basil, oregano,
   marjoram, thyme, etc.)
1 cup (250 mL) canned navy, cannelini
   or white kidney beans
salt and pepper to taste

BREADING
5–7 rye Swedish style crackers,
   crushed to a fine powder
1 tsp (5 mL) onion powder
1 tsp (5 mL) garlic powder
1 tsp (5 mL) celery powder
1 tsp (5 mL) parsley flakes
salt and pepper to taste

Preheat oven to 400°F (200°C).

Put the olive oil, garlic and onion into a pan and cook on high heat until the onions are translucent. I use a little oil to start and then I add some of the potato water as needed. When it's cooked, remove it from the heat and set it aside.

Slice or dice the vegetarian ham or pepperoni. Put the potatoes through a potato ricer or mash them coarsely with a fork. Add the pepperoni, onion/garlic mixture, parsley and Italian seasoning. Mash the beans with a fork or blend them as desired. Add them into the potato mixture and gently mix the whole thing.

Mix together the ingredients for the breading in a bowl. Put a piece of parchment on a baking sheet and perhaps lightly olive oil it as well. Now it gets fun.

Form the potato mixture into balls. I think the originals were a little bigger than golf balls. The ones I make are about 4 inches (10 cm) long and sort of egg-shaped. Gently roll them in the breading mixture to coat them well. Then put them on a baking sheet lightly coated with oil or covered in parchment. Bake until they're crispy and hot. This should take 20–25 minutes, depending on the heat of your oven.

This would be good with Killer Tomato Salad (page 34) and some Carrot-Lemon Zinger (page 27). That would get your taste buds going in a few different directions.

This meal isn't complex, but there are a lot of steps. If you're making it for company, why not make it a day ahead, then bake it when your guests arrive? Never stress yourself out!

I had a vegan cooking class to teach and we were having a long, rainy cold spell. I wanted to give them a naughty-tasting, rich dish that could be easily prepared and cure everyone of the winter blues. It worked well—everyone said they'd make it at home.

Preheat oven to 425°F (220°C).

Oil a medium baking pan and then add the remaining oil to the pan. Peel any vegetable you don't like the peel on and then coarsely chop the vegetables. Place them in the pan, adding about half the soy milk and the other ingredients and toss it all well. Bake it at 400°F (200°C) for about 45 minutes, or until it's fork-tender. You should check the veggies along the way, turning them if they're browned, or adding more soy milk or water if it's all cooked off.

When everything is cooked through, coarsely mash it with a fork, or use a hand blender to break up everything to a smoother consistency, then add more soy milk or seasonings as you wish. Prepare another pan, olive-oiled or lined in parchment. If you use parchment, make sure it goes up the sides, or put olive oil up the sides. Lay the potato mixture across the bottom, spreading it evenly.

Sauté the onions, garlic and peppers in the olive oil in a pan. Stir constantly on medium-high, turning the heat down if it starts to stick. You can add a bit of water if needed. Continue cooking until the onions are translucent. Add the mushrooms, parsley and green onions and continue cooking until the mushrooms cook down somewhat. Add the vegetarian ground "beef," stirring well. Add the tomato sauce and continue to cook, reducing the heat to a simmer. Add the oregano, cinnamon, salt, pepper and hot sauce if desired. Thin with more water if necessary (it should be like a thick spaghetti sauce).

Spread the Sloppy Joe mixture over the potato mixture and serve. Or you can bake it in the oven for about 20–25 minutes at 400°F (200°C) to combine the flavors even more and heat through.

FOR THE CASSEROLE BASE:
2 Tbsp (30 mL) olive oil
3 large baking potatoes
1 large carrot
1 parsnip, sweet potato or yam
1 large onion
6 cloves garlic, finely chopped
1 cup (250 mL) unsweetened soy milk
½ tsp (2 mL) salt
½ tsp (2 mL) pepper
½ tsp (2 mL) nutmeg

SLOPPY JOE TOPPING
2 Tbsp (30 mL) olive oil
2 onions, chopped
1 bulb garlic, finely chopped
1 green pepper, chopped
1 red pepper, chopped
5–6 crimini (brown) mushrooms, sliced
½ cup (125 mL) flat-leaf parsley, chopped
2 green onions, finely chopped
11-oz (312-g) package of vegetarian ground "beef"
1 cup (250 mL) tomato sauce
1 tsp (5 mL) oregano
pinch of cinnamon
salt and pepper to taste
a few dashes of hot sauce (optional)

Sweet Potato Pecan Puffs

SERVES 4–6

I devised these for a holiday meal when I didn't feel like making a dish with regular potatoes. I just wanted something different and these work well, especially if you're serving a bunch of people. They're equally good piping hot or at room temperature. They can sit on a plate as you bring in other dishes with no loss of quality.

2 medium sweet potatoes, finely chopped
6 cloves garlic, chopped
1 cup (250 mL) unsweetened soy milk
1 Tbsp (15 mL) extra virgin olive oil
2 cups (500 mL) toasted pecans, chopped
2 green onions, finely chopped
1 cup (250 mL) parsley, finely chopped
sprigs of fresh basil and sage, finely chopped
salt and pepper to taste
pinch nutmeg (optional)

Preheat oven to 400°F (200°C).

Put the sweet potatoes into a large pot with the garlic and cover with water. Bring to a boil, cover and turn down to medium heat. Cook until the sweet potatoes are fork-tender, enough that they can be mashed.

Mash with a fork, hand blender, potato masher or ricer. They can be smooth as silk or a little chunky, depending on your mood. Then, simply add the soy milk, olive oil, half the pecans, the onions, herbs and seasonings. You can pipe them onto a parchment-covered baking sheet with a piping bag fitted with a large tip if you want to get fancy. Or you can spoon them on. Of course, the bigger you make them, the longer they'll take to brown, so keep that in mind.

Sprinkle the rest of the pecans on top, pressing them in lightly so they won't burn.

Cook these for about 25 minutes, or until they're golden brown. Remember, they're already cooked—you just have to brown them.

Pecans are festive—but you could use any nut you like with these.

Paula Deen, whose show "Paula's Home Cooking" is a fave of mine, cooks with pecans. She also says "pe-cans," unlike most southerners I've met who say "pe-cons." Check her out; she's a blast.

These make a fun addition to Thanksgiving or Christmas dinners. Enjoy these served on your holiday plate, alongside a bed of beautiful organic greens and a mountain of stuffing.

I prepared these on a TV show once, and the crew loved them. Probably because of the fresh sage, they kept referring to them as "stuffing cookies."

Carboholic Fantasy

SERVES 4–6

I asked a friend what he was eating one day and he said, "Noodles and mashed potatoes." And I thought I loved carbs! Never had I done noodles and potatoes together—but it sounded cool. That was the inspiration for this dish, a pasta dish with a potato sauce. So much for moderation.

30-oz (900-g) package fettuccine
4 medium yellow potatoes, peeled
   and finely chopped
1 Tbsp (15 mL) olive oil
1 large onion, finely chopped
4 cloves garlic, finely chopped
1 stalk celery, finely chopped
½ cup (125 mL) unsweetened soy milk
2 Tbsp (30 mL) fresh thyme, finely chopped
1 cup (250 mL) flat-leaf parsley, finely chopped
½ cup (125 mL) white wine or dry sherry (optional)
salt and lots of freshly cracked black pepper

Boil a large pot of water and throw in the potatoes. When they're cooked through, remove them and drain, saving the water for the pasta.

Put the olive oil, onion, garlic and celery into a pan and cook on high, stirring constantly. Add a bit of the pasta water if it starts to stick. Cook until the onions are translucent and then remove from the heat. Add the potatoes and the soy milk. Mash the mixture well, then whisk or whiz up with a hand blender to a sauce-like consistency.

Bring the water (from the potatoes) to a full rolling boil. Add the fettucine and cook according to the package.

Meanwhile, put the potato sauce on low and add the thyme and parsley. Add the wine or sherry if desired, a bit at a time, so as not to thin it too much. Keep the sauce at a low simmer until it's ready to use. Drain the pasta when it's done and lightly toss it in olive oil. Taste and season the sauce lightly with salt. Serve the pasta with the parsley, red pepper, carrot and green onion on the side. Pour the gorgeous sauce over the top of each plate. Finish with freshly cracked black pepper and dive in!

You could use colored pasta if you wanted to visually wake up this plate. I figured the stuff on the side would be enough. You don't want to mess too much with the "taboo" quality of this dish!

I said I had never done noodles and potatoes, but I HAVE made gnocchi—pasta with a potato base, and one of my favorite things on earth. Another carboholic's dream dish.

You can use this potato sauce as a gravy for anything—and since potatoes pick up flavors, it will make a great base.

V CUISINE

Curry is kind of like discussing religion and politics—you either love it or you hate it. I never had the stuff until I was around 18 years old and I instantly became a fan. I loved it so much I wanted it in EVERYTHING. If I opened a can of soup I had to dump curry into it. Luckily my curry taste buds have become a bit more refined over the years.

Curry is actually a spice blend that can encompass many different spices. Each kind can be very different in character. Some are mild and earthy, others are pungent, with deep, heated notes, but not actually hot. Some are hellishly fiery!

I love the intensity of the spices and I love the fresh things you can pair with curry for contrast. You can use literally any vegetable, bean or grain and have endless meals with different personalities. I particularly love that the vegetarian versions are as terrific as their meat counterparts.

When I'm not sure what to prepare, I know I can always pull out a few ingredients and throw together a curry. Since curries are awesome slowly simmered, they're perfect to make in slow cookers. Throw it together the night before, then come home to a creamy, dreamy pot of aromatic curry. Serve it with basmati rice, or a whole grain, some pita bread or roti and there you go. Brilliant!

I'm very prejudiced in this area—I'm a curry FREAK! If you haven't discovered curries yet, I hope I'm the one to turn you onto them. If you don't like it at all, there may not be hope—it's just one of those things. For those who do enjoy these exotic flavors, go wild!

COURAGEOUS CURRIES

Tomato Curried Lentils

This is a nice, tangy dish with the delightful POW of curry to wake up bored taste buds. I like this served over a whole grain. Quinoa is fluffy and absorbs the sauce, yet with more bite—it's perfect!

2 Tbsp (30 mL) olive oil

1 large onion, chopped

1 stalk celery, finely chopped

several cloves of garlic, finely chopped

2 cups (500 mL) lentils

2 cups (500 mL) unsweetened soy milk

1 cup (250 mL) tomato sauce

1 cup (250 mL) flat-leaf parsley, finely chopped

1 tsp (5 mL) ground cumin

2 tsp (10 mL) curry powder or paste of your choice

salt and pepper to taste

hot sauce or cayenne pepper (depending on the heat of your curry)

1 cup (250 mL) cherry or grape tomatoes

3 cups (750 mL) cooked quinoa

Put the olive oil, onion and celery into a pot, on high heat. Stirring constantly, cook until the onions are translucent, about 3–4 minutes. Add the garlic and lentils, and cover them with water. Turn the heat down to medium, cover it and let the curry simmer. The lentils have to soften—just make sure you don't run out of water.

When the lentils are cooked (about half an hour) and most of the water is gone, add the other ingredients except the cherry tomatoes. Simmer uncovered on medium-low for another half an hour if possible, or longer. About 5 minutes before removing from the heat, add the tomatoes.

Serve over quinoa, basmati rice or any other grain of your choice.

The Incas called quinoa "the mother grain." It's a high protein, easy-to-cook ancient grain that's making a comeback. Try some today.

After this curry is done, you could (instead of serving it over a grain), add two more cups of unsweetened soy milk and have it as a spicy soup. Delicious!

Quinoa conains a close-to-perfect combination of 8 amino acids for tissue development in humans.

Fresh Tomato Onion Chutney

SERVES 4–6

You may not consider this your idea of chutney, but many Indian and Fijian people do. I have to have this with curries. It tastes amazingly fresh and looks magnificent. It cuts right through the heat of a hot curry and livens up your mouth. Yum! You can't have a boring plate with bright red, green and crisp white—it's impossible.

2 tomatoes, chopped
1 onion, finely chopped
2 cups (500 mL) cilantro, finely chopped
salt to taste
optional: drizzle olive oil, vinegar or both

Combine the ingredients, tossing lightly. That's it; it's as easy as can be and carries a big impact.

Try this as a salad along with anything you want. Its fresh, fragrant zip goes well with a lot of foods, especially spicy ones.

Cilantro is another of those ya-either-love-it-or-hate-it things. If you don't salivate over cilantro, replace it with parsley. Flat-leaf parsley still gives you that fresh green bite without the pungent taste.

Let's face it—if you have this chutney leftover, you might as well add it to a soup, stew or stir-fry. The tomatoes will be watery after a few hours. However, I've never had any leftover!

For a complete departure from the usual, get the little green tomatillos instead of or along with the red tomatoes. They're hard to get where I live, but if you can obtain them, try it with this! Tomatillos are delectable.

Creative Cauliflower Curry with Chickpeas

Mmmm! This is for when you want bold flavors—nothing wimpy here. There's nothing like doing something super energetic and having a big curry dinner as the ultimate reward.

Put 1 Tbsp (15 mL) of olive oil into a hot pan, adding more as needed. Add the onion and garlic. Cook, stirring constantly on high heat until the onions are translucent. Add all the whole spices and stir rapidly. Add the cauliflower, red pepper, zucchini and potatoes and cover them with the soy milk and enough water to cover. Put a lid on the pot and simmer on low until the vegetables are tender. When they are, add the chickpeas and curry, salt and pepper, cayenne and hot spice if desired. Last, toss in the parsley or peas.

Taste, adjust seasonings, and serve. It's awesome over basmati rice, any whole grain, wrapped in a roti, over pasta or toast or even plain—like a rich stew. Make sure you have some Fresh Tomato Onion Chutney (page 99) on hand, and if possible make Greens to Go with Curry (page 102) as well.

If you wish, you can remove the cinnamon stick, cardamom pods, etc. They'll be bitter if you bite into them. Some people hate the whole spices in curry and others love to suck on them (I do). Just use caution with kids and people who inhale their food.

2 Tbsp (30 mL) olive oil
1 onion, finely chopped
1 bulb garlic, finely chopped
½ cinnamon stick, broken
1 tsp (5 mL) coriander seed
½ tsp (2 mL) whole cloves
1 tsp (5 mL) cardamom pods
1 heaping tsp (5 mL) fennel seeds
½ tsp (2 mL) mustard seeds
4 or 5 whole star anise
2 tsp (10 mL) cumin seeds
2 cups (500 mL) cauliflower, cut into florettes
½ red pepper, chopped
1 zucchini, chopped
4–5 small potatoes, cut into quarters
1–2 cups (250–500 mL) unsweetened soy milk
1 cup (250 mL) chickpeas (canned or cooked)
1 Tbsp (15 mL) madras curry powder
salt and pepper
cayenne pepper, hot peppers or hot sauce (optional)
1 cup (250 mL) chopped parsley or frozen peas

If you want a thicker curry, remove the lid and continue to cook it on low until it reaches the desired consistency. The potatoes will work as a thickening agent.

If you can get curry leaves (available at Indian markets and some specialty markets), by all means, buy some. Add them at the beginning of the simmering process for added flavor.

Greens to Go with Curry

These bright, flavorful greens accompany curries perfectly. Pick an assortment of greens to your taste: spinach, beet leaves, collards, mustard or dandelion greens, escarole, rapini, etc. Use as much as will fit into the pot you're using; they'll cook way down with the heat. I've given you fairly tame amounts here, but you could cook more. They're delectable; they'll get eaten.

2 Tbsp (30 mL) olive oil
1 onion, finely chopped
garlic, several cloves, finely chopped
1 tsp (5 mL) mustard seeds
½ tsp (2 mL) fenugreek
½ tsp (2 mL) coriander
6 cups greens
½ tsp (2 mL) ground cardamom
1 tsp (5 mL) ground cumin
salt and pepper to taste

Put the olive oil into a pan and add in the onion and garlic, stirring constantly on medium heat. Pop in the mustard seeds, fenugreek and coriander and cook until the onions are translucent. Add the greens and stir madly. Add a bit more olive oil or other liquid in small amounts at a time, constantly stirring. Add the cardamom and cumin. When the greens cook down a bit and are a brighter, more intense green, remove from the heat.

The greens have a ton of flavor alone but the additions here really give them an extra kick. They complement creamy, spicy curries and somehow contrast them, although they contain some of the same spices.

As for color, these will really jazz up a plate. Green things have a way of doing that. I also like to have Fresh Tomato Onion Chutney (page 99) and some basmati rice or a roti to roll it all up in. This is great dinner party fare. Everything can be ready in advance and kept warm. That way you don't have to miss a second of socializing.

If you're cooking more than one variety of greens, make sure to add in the tougher greens first, as they'll need to cook longer. Something like rapini, which has a stalk, will need to cook longer than spinach, which is leafy.

Romance is in the air! Cleopatra is said to have adored the scent of cardamom and when Marc Anthony would come to visit, she'd have the palace filled with cardamom smoke.

Ravishing Roti

These are the perfect complement to an Indian meal. They may be easier to make than you think. These little pancakes can wrap up curry ingredients for flavor and portability. You can put any sort of sandwich ingredients in them and they'll be fresh and delicious.

3 cups whole wheat flour
1 Tbsp (15 mL) olive oil
1 tsp (5 mL) salt
1½ cups (375 mL) hot water

Simply mix together all of the ingredients. When they're well incorporated and soft, knead the dough a few times. Make about 14 balls out of the dough. Roll them out so that each looks about the size of a small tortilla.

Heat the pan to medium-high with just a tiny amount of oil, enough to barely coat the pan when you spread it with a pancake turner, or, as I like to call it, a flipper. When the oil is hot, add the roti. Leave it there for about 10 seconds and then flip it. It should have fine bubbles in the top and have the edges starting to firm up. Between each flip, refresh with a dot of olive oil, as necessary.

Pile them up as you finish each, and keep them wrapped in foil to keep them from drying out. You can keep them warm in the oven until you're ready to use them.

These are perfect filled with anything curried, or really anything you want to stuff them with. Try a small line of basmati rice, a little hot curry sauce and some Fresh Tomato Onion Chutney (page 99).

If you don't have time to make roti, sometimes you can find frozen ones at the supermarket, or at an Indian market. Or find some good tortilla wraps, wrap them in foil and bake at 325°F (160°C) until warm.

You can bake these instead of frying: Lay parchment paper over a baking sheet and put the roti on top of that. Then cover it with foil, almost flat against the roti, and either tuck it in (if the sheet is flat) or go right to the edge if the sheet has sides. Bake at 350°F (180°C) for about 10 minutes. This will cook it like a soft flour tortilla. If you want browning, take off the foil, lightly oil it if desired and put it under the broiler until golden brown, flipping when done on one side. Repeat on the other side.

V CUISINE

In V Cuisine, a side dish is basically anything you want to be a side dish. You could easily spin any of these into a main course. Here I call them side dishes because their main component is vegetables, as opposed to a heavy-duty protein. And although I actually do serve these as side dishes, I would never promise to conform to such a thing. I enjoy breaking my own rules as much as the next person.

The way I usually pick a side dish is by color. If I'm serving something brown, and something yellow, the side dish will have to be red or green. There's nothing worse than a dull plate—like hospital food. In fact, I always try to serve something bright green, if not in a side dish, then certainly in a salad. Failing that, a little pile of parsley on the plate is nice, especially if you eat it.

Or you might want to pick a side dish on the basis of texture. If you're having some mashed sweet potatoes and baked tofu, you need something with a bit of snap! How about lightly stir-fried snow peas and a sprinkling of almonds, with a few raw red pepper slices? Gorgeous!

I make a lot of one-pot meals, so don't always do side dishes. I do like to have several different experiences on one plate though, and side dishes are a great way to achieve that. Simple ones tend to be best.

I hope you try some of these recipes. Remember, if you have no time to cook an extra dish, just cut up a few raw veggies and throw them on the plate. That's enough color, contrast and interest for anyone.

SUPER SIDES!

Mushrooms Giya

SERVES 4

This is a takeoff of an Old World Italian salad. I named this dish after my all-time favorite aunt. I don't know if she even likes mushrooms, but it sounded good. She's Italian, a lot of fun and always fed me things I adored.

12 crimini mushrooms, sliced thinly

2 Tbsp (30 mL) extra virgin olive oil

¼ cup (60 mL) lemon juice

1 sweet onion (Vidalia would be good) thinly
   sliced and pulled apart (in rings)

4 stalks celery, thinly sliced across, so there
   are hundreds of little "moons"

a few celery leaves, finely chopped

½ cup (125 mL) parsley, finely chopped

salt and freshly cracked pepper to taste

¼ cup (60 mL) blanched almonds, crushed or slivered
   to sprinkle on top

Put all of the ingredients (except the almonds if you're using them) in a good-sized bowl and gently mix them together. Cover and let the mixture sit for at least half an hour so the flavors can mix. To serve, put this on a beautiful plate and sprinkle with almonds if desired.

This dish makes a wonderful meal by itself, or served with some really great bread. You could take this mixture and put it on top of a freshly baked, thin crust pizza. It would look fantastic on a bed of spinach or steamed collard greens. It would be fantastic on polenta. Wow!

This is also a gorgeous starter for a special meal. Arrange a plate with a few crisp leaves of butter lettuce (or, even better, radicchio), a handful of cherry tomatoes and this very sumptuous mushroom creation.

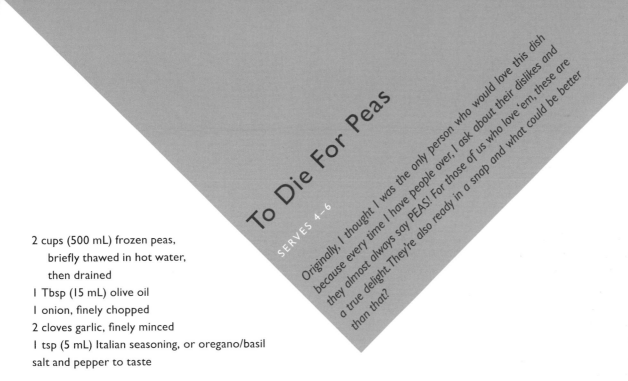

To Die For Peas

SERVES 4-6

Originally, I thought I was the only person who would love this dish because every time I have people over, I ask about their dislikes and they almost always say PEAS! For those of us who love 'em, these are a true delight. They're also ready in a snap and what could be better than that?

2 cups (500 mL) frozen peas,
   briefly thawed in hot water,
   then drained
1 Tbsp (15 mL) olive oil
1 onion, finely chopped
2 cloves garlic, finely minced
1 tsp (5 mL) Italian seasoning, or oregano/basil
salt and pepper to taste

Put the olive oil, garlic and onion in a hot pan and stir for a minute or two. Add the peas and seasoning and cook for a couple of minutes more, but not long enough to lose the vibrant green color. You could also just take the onion and garlic mixture off of the heat and toss in the cold peas, that way you won't have any loss of color or nutrients.

You can do endless variations on this theme. You could do this exactly the same way, except to replace the Italian seasoning with a little bit of curry powder. Yum! Or give it a squirt of hot sauce or whatever seasoning you're into.

Nigella Lawson, the TV cook and domestic goddess, advocates the use of frozen peas in many of her recipes. I agree. She makes "mushy peas" (reconstituted frozen peas, blended up and seasoned) as a bright side dish. She throws them into all manner of other dishes. It's a fast cooking item to add flavor, color and nutrition.

Popsicle Peas – There are some kids who wouldn't touch a cooked pea on a plate, but they're quite overjoyed about eating "popsicle peas" straight out of the freezer. This also applies to "popsicle" corn.

A little bit of fresh ginger added to split peas while cooking helps to preserve their color.

Cold Steamed Asparagus Ambrosia

SERVES 4–8

One of my friends and I have an obsession with roasted garlic, roasted red peppers and artichokes. We want them on everything. They're deadly good on pizza, in crispy sandwiches or on any salad. And let's not forget on pasta. Try fresh whole wheat or spelt linguine, with a light tomato sauce. Then top that with a shocking amount of roasted garlic, the peppers and the artichokes—food of the gods!

1 bunch asparagus
1 full roasted red pepper
   (or several pieces from a jar)
1 bulb roasted garlic (see page 57)
1 cup (250 mL) marinated artichoke hearts
1 clove garlic, finely minced
2 Tbsp (30 mL) extra virgin olive oil
1 tsp (5 mL) honey† or sugar
1 Tbsp (15 mL) light vinegar
salt and pepper to taste
1 head butter lettuce
finely chopped fresh parsley, or green onions, for garnish

Break off the fibrous ends of the asparagus and discard. Place in a steamer set on high for about 5 minutes or until fork-tender. They should be a beautiful vivid green and still have some firmness to the spears. If desired, plunge the asparagus into cold water to stop the cooking process and maintain the color. Drain, cut into 1–2 inch (2.5–5 cm) pieces and set aside.

Cut the red peppers into strips and add them to a bowl along with the garlic and artichokes. In a separate bowl, whisk the remaining ingredients together, add them to the bowl and toss well.

Rinse and dry the lettuce, rip it into bite-sized pieces and arrange it on a platter.

Turn out the asparagus mixture onto the bed of butter lettuce. If you like, sprinkle the dish with the finely chopped parsley or several green onions.

† **VEGAN OPTION** agave syrup, brown rice syrup or barley malt syrup

When cooking asparagus in water, always use that water to make a soup or stew—it's loaded with the vitamins.

The tiny, delicate asparagus stalks are best. They're tender and sometimes quite sweet, although they still possess the unique flavor of asparagus.

Due to its cold nature, this dish is ideal for a hot day. There's plenty going on in it to perk you up. Pair it with more light foods, or eat it by itself.

Plain asparagus, lightly steamed and then doused in fresh lemon can be fantastic. It's light, but at the same time surprisingly filling.

Bold Broiled Eggplant

SERVES 4

When I was a kid, if someone had told me I'd be madly in love with eggplant one day, I never would have believed it. My husband was revolted by the stuff as a kid too, and now he's totally into it. But then, we probably never had it this way back then.

1 large, deep purple eggplant
½ cup (125 mL) olive oil
¼ cup (60 mL) balsamic vinegar
¼ cup (60 mL) soy sauce
1 tsp (5 mL) salt
½ tsp (2 mL) pepper
1 tsp (5 mL) garlic, finely minced
½ tsp (2 mL) onion powder
1 tsp (5 mL) oregano
1 Tbsp lemon juice

Cut the eggplant into large rounds about ¼–½ inches (6 mm–1 cm) thick. Take all the other ingredients and mix them together well. Olive oil a baking sheet, or use parchment—it's better for clean-up. Place the eggplant rounds on the sheet. Turn the broiler on high. Brush or spoon on the mixture and spread it liberally on each round. Place the rounds under the broiler. There's no way around this; you'll have to watch them because they only take a few minutes to cook.

The eggplant will become golden brown (my husband likes his black and actually refers to this dish as "blackened eggplant"). There's one in every crowd who likes things charred, but I don't recommend it. You'll see the middles become kind of translucent looking and then firm up under the broiler. There should be some sizzling from the oil.

When they look great (firm/golden around the edges), flip them over. Brush or spoon the mixture onto the other side. Then back under the broiler they go. When they look just as tasty as the other side, remove them from the heat and serve.

I serve this dish as is for an appetizer, sometimes with bread on the side to soak up the juice.

My favorite way to serve this is to remove the eggplant from the heat, cut it into strips and then serve it over pasta with a light tomato sauce. It works with any kind of pasta, of course, but I like fettuccine or shells with this. A friend of mine and I adored this concoction when we were both pregnant and in total eating mode. We'd shop till we dropped, then go to my place and whip this up.

Eggplant is another food that Thomas Jefferson is credited to have introduced to the U.S. It's surprising that he did, since eggplant was feared to cause madness and a multitude of diseases. It wasn't widely accepted in Europe or North America, almost right up until the 20th century.

Black Beauty Beans with Spicy Green Olives

SERVES 4–6

Season this in many different ways, depending on your mood. It can be ultra spicy or completely mellow. You can give it a Tex-Mex feel or a European flair. It's as delicious heated up or as I've presented it here, served at room temperature.

1½ cups (375 mL) canned black
    beans, drained and rinsed
¾ cup (175 mL) spicy manzanilla
    (big, green) olives,
    cut in half or smaller
½ cup (125 mL) finely sliced roasted
    red, or fresh red peppers
¼ cup (60 mL) fresh parsley,
    finely chopped
1 green onion, finely chopped
½ tsp (2 mL) onion powder
½ tsp (2 mL) paprika
½ tsp (2 mL) basil
½ tsp (2 mL) ground rosemary
salt and pepper to taste
red pepper flakes (optional)
drizzle of extra virgin olive oil (optional)

Simply combine all of the above ingredients in a bowl and toss them. This makes a super attractive and very complete meal served atop a bed of fresh lettuce. It also looks and tastes amazing against anything made of corn like polenta or corn bread.

Serve this alongside a bright red tomato salad, covered in rings of red onion—to liven you up.

To do the corn and bean thing up right, how about making some cornbread stuffing to go with this? It's down-home food at its best.

Black beans have plenty of protein and fiber. They're great for energy and you won't be hungry after eating them. Dietary fiber combats many of the worst health concerns. North Americans only get about half as much as they should. Beans can be part of the solution.

Steamed Carrots in Lemon Sauce

SERVES 4–6

These carrots are elegant, delicious and decadent. Most people have never experienced this particular dish. I'd serve these with rice, mushrooms and a big spinach salad. A brown and wild rice pilaf would be terrific. This is a treat for the eye, and tastes as great as it looks.

LEMON SAUCE

2 Tbsp (30 mL) olive oil

1 large onion, finely chopped

1 heaping Tbsp (15 mL) unbleached white flour

2 cups (500 mL) lemon juice

1 Tbsp (15 mL) lemon rind, finely grated

Put the olive oil and the onion in a pan on high, stirring constantly. Add the flour and whisk it in; the mixture will be lumpy. Keep stirring and cook it. Then add a little bit of lemon juice and continue cooking and whisking the mixture. Keep adding the lemon juice and whisking until all the juice is used. Remove it from the stove and blend it with an upright or hand blender until it's smooth and silky. Return it to the pan and add the grated lemon rind. Keep it on low heat until it's ready to use, stirring occasionally. This sauce is translucent and not too thick.

CARROTS

3–4 large carrots, cut into rounds

¼ cup (60 mL) fresh parsley, finely chopped

salt and pepper to taste

1 lemon, cut into rounds

Steam the carrots until they're fork-tender. Put them in a bowl or on a beautiful platter. Sprinkle the carrots with the parsley, salt and pepper and then pour the lemon sauce over them liberally. Arrange the lemon rounds on top

Not just a myth: carrots are good for your eyesight, especially night vision. It's the Vitamin A that does it.

The Romans were great cookers of carrots, making elaborate soups and dressing them in wine, oil and spices.

Colorful Fall Steamed Veggies with Sage Sauce

SERVES 6.

You can find some great vegetables in the fall. This dish is perfect for root vegetables any time. Other than a bit of cutting, it won't stress you out. I use this as a main course or a side dish—it's good either way. I would also double the recipe to have extra for later in the week.

2 carrots, coarsely chopped

1 parsnip, coarsely chopped

3 potatoes, quartered

1 turnip, chopped

1 red pepper, cut into small pieces (1 inch or so)

1 green pepper, chopped

1 small butternut squash, washed and chopped

SAGE SAUCE

1 piece each of the above carrot, parsnip, potato and turnip

¾ cup (175 mL) soy milk

1 tsp (5 mL) sage

1 tsp (5 mL) olive oil (optional)

salt and pepper to taste

Put all the vegetables into a steamer and cook on high heat for 5–10 minutes or until fork-tender. You could also boil them, which is okay and delightfully fat-free. Whenever possible, steam food to retain its flavor and vitamin content; if you do boil, though, save that broth to make flavorful stocks, gravies, sauces, etc.

Blend up the above sauce ingredients with an upright or hand blender. Make sure it's smooth. If you need more liquid, add a bit of white wine or the water from boiling or steaming. Put the sauce in a small saucepan, bring it to a boil and cook it on low until it reaches the desired consistency (like heavy cream or thicker). Taste for seasoning and add more sage if you like. Fresh sage leaves are all the better and you can purée them along with the rest.

Parsnips contain Vitamin C, iron, calcium and fiber. They're a great addition to soups and stews and have a distinct flavor, yet absorb other flavors.

A great way to serve this dish is in a shallow bowl on a bed of steamed beet leaves or raw spinach. Place the hot steamed vegetables on the greens. If you use spinach, the heat of the vegetables will cook it a bit. Pour the sage sauce over the top and serve it immediately. This would be a super hearty meal for a cold autumn day, maybe after a hike or a hayride.

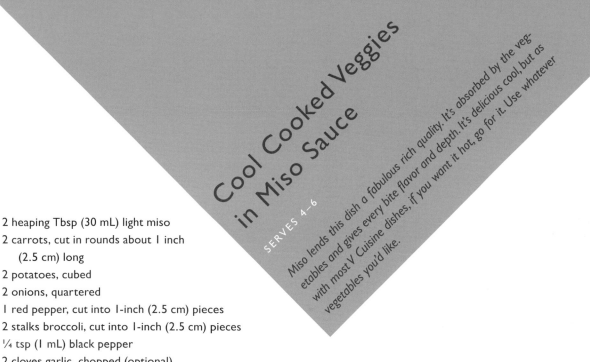

Cool Cooked Veggies in Miso Sauce

SERVES 4–6

Miso lends this dish a fabulous rich quality. It's absorbed by the vegetables and gives every bite flavor and depth. It's delicious cool, but as with most V Cuisine dishes, if you want it hot, go for it. Use whatever vegetables you'd like.

2 heaping Tbsp (30 mL) light miso
2 carrots, cut in rounds about 1 inch
   (2.5 cm) long
2 potatoes, cubed
2 onions, quartered
1 red pepper, cut into 1-inch (2.5 cm) pieces
2 stalks broccoli, cut into 1-inch (2.5 cm) pieces
¼ tsp (1 mL) black pepper
2 cloves garlic, chopped (optional)

Put the above ingredients into a covered pot on medium heat with about 2 cups (500 mL) of water. Cook them until the vegetables are tender. The liquid should be reduced by at least half and thickened quite a bit. If your pot has such a happening lid that it doesn't allow any liquid to get out, remove it to achieve this. Then, remove the pot from the heat, cover it and refrigerate it for about 15 minutes.

Notice I didn't add salt to this recipe. That's because most miso is incredibly salty and it shouldn't be necessary. But you can taste it and decide for yourself; every miso has a different character and it all depends on how it interacts with the veggies you choose.

This is wonderful served on a large platter and sprinkled with finely chopped parsley or sprinkled with toasted sesame or flaxseeds. You could serve this with a vegetable-laden pasta salad. This dish makes a healthful, light, flavorful lunch.

You could take your cooked veggies and put the entire thing into a blender or food processor and blend it until it's smooth. This may require additional liquid. You could add rice vinegar, water, white wine, soy milk or a combination of those. Then you would have a beautiful base for soups, sauces, dressings, etc.

Broccoli is great stuff. In addition to great taste, it offers medicinal value toward fighting ulcers and cancer.

Whole grains are the sweethearts of the carbohydrate world. I'd never tell you to eat a donut, but I do believe these dishes, which are full of GOOD carbs, are something you should be turned on to. Some whole grains are brown rice, quinoa, spelt, kamut and wheat and rye berries. I hope you'll expand your knowledge of whole grains and try them all.

What's great about them? Well, the living part of the grain, the endosperm, is still intact. The hull hasn't been removed or the grain polished, so the vitamins are basically there and the bran and germ remain as well.

This means that they contain more dietary fiber, antioxidants and protein than refined carbohydrates. Whole grains contain minerals (selenium, magnesium, manganese and phosphorus) and vitamins (niacin, thiamin, riboflavin and Vitamin B6). There's evidence that they prevent some cancers, heart disease, obesity and diabetes.

Push all that aside and I have two other great reasons to eat whole grains: they have amazing flavor and texture. The best part of all is that they have food value; they give your body fuel and energy for your insanely busy day. The first thing I noticed when I began really eating whole grains was the endless energy I had. I love that, since I have tons to accomplish in a day and can't stand dragging myself around.

I can honestly say that I would choose a whole grain over a refined carb a huge portion of the time. The texture's more interesting. It's like going back to white bread (ick!) once you're used to rich, brown bread.

Whole grains satisfy your carbohydrate cravings. You may want a cookie, but if you have ½ cup of a whole grain, flavored the way you like, it will do the trick.

GUILTLESS GRAINS

Wild Rice with Heavenly Hazelnut Sauce

SERVES 4–6

Wild rice is excellent. It really isn't rice; it's a grain, so better yet. It's pretty expensive, so most people only have it in a pilaf. Some is better than none. I love it as the star of a dish. There's something special about this long black grain that's excitingly different. Pair it with this hazelnut sauce and you'll fly into the wild blue yonder!

2 cups (500 mL) wild rice
1 red pepper, finely diced
1 green pepper, finely diced
3 green onions, finely chopped
½ cup (125 mL) parsley or cilantro, finely chopped

HEAVENLY HAZELNUT SAUCE
2 Tbsp (30 mL) olive oil
1 large onion, finely chopped
1 green onion, finely chopped
4 cloves garlic, finely chopped
2 Tbsp (30 mL) flour
3 cups (750 mL) unsweetened soy milk
2 Tbsp (30 mL) dry sherry
1 cup (250 mL) hazelnuts, crushed
salt and pepper to taste

Boil 5 cups (1.25L) of water in a pot and then add the rice. Cover it, turn the heat down to low and boil/steam that way until the water is cooked off, about 20–25 minutes. The rice will be tender through but still have some bite to it. Take the red and green pepper, green onion and parsley or cilantro and add them to the rice pot when it's hot, but the rice is done cooking. That way they'll steam a bit on the rice, but still have some crunch. Keep it covered until you serve it.

Put the olive oil in a pan, heat it to high and add the onion, green onion and garlic, stirring them constantly until the onions are translucent. Turn the heat down to medium and add the flour.

Whisk constantly until the flour begins to cook, then add a little bit of the soy milk and continue to whisk it. Keep adding the soy milk, slowly, until the sauce has the consistency of heavy cream. Add the sherry if desired. Add the hazelnuts. Turn the heat to low and continue to simmer it for at least 10 minutes. If the sauce gets too thick, add more soy milk or a little bit of water and whisk it again. Keep an eye on it constantly so that it doesn't stick (this shouldn't be a problem if the heat is low). The hazelnuts will soften and the entire sauce will improve as the flavors meld.

Remove the sauce from the heat and cool it a bit. Completely purée the sauce or if you want the sauce chunky then you can leave it. Heat the sauce up to hot again and then serve it immediately.

When removing the rice from the pan, stir in the veggies you added. Season it with salt and pepper.

Try this with something ultra green like a beautiful spinach dish, some bright green rapini or a huge helping of gai-lan or broccoli. All your nutrients are in one place—tons of protein in the wild rice and hazelnuts (also calcium in the nuts) and fiber in the greens.

There is evidence (through Chinese writings) that the hazelnut has been around in some form for 4,500 years. It was considered one of the 5 sacred nourishments delivered by God to humans.

Ancient texts say that hazelnuts were used to mash into a paste to put over a scorpion bite. And the leaves were believed to be a blood purifier.

Festive Orange Rice

SERVES 4–6

Here's a dish that's V Cuisine at its best. It's got great taste, great color and it's good for you. You'll never feel deprived eating fresh bright flavors like this. What's really fun about this dish is that it goes amazingly with almost anything. You can use it with Mediterranean fare, with Chinese food and just as well alongside any North American dish. It's a better alternative any time you would normally serve plain rice.

3 cups rice (brown basmati works well)
1 cup (250 mL) orange juice concentrate
salt and pepper to taste
½ cup (125 mL) orange juice
1 orange, cut into rounds
parsley to garnish

Preheat oven to 350°F (180°C).

Bring 6 cups (1.5 L) of water to a boil. Add the brown rice. Add the orange juice concentrate and then turn down the heat to low, simmering slowly. Cover until ready. Taste the rice to see if it's done. It'll have more texture than soft, white rice. When ready, remove it from the heat and keep it covered. It's okay if it's slightly undercooked since you're going to bake it. Add salt and pepper if desired.

Gently stir in the orange juice.

Lightly olive oil a 9-inch (2.5-L) square or a 9-inch (2.5-L) round pan. Fill it with the cooked rice. Place the orange slices over the top. Bake the rice until it's warmed through. This usually takes about 20–30 minutes. Garnish with the parsley. You'll end up with an orange infused rice dish—*mmmm!*—and the aroma will perfume your kitchen.

This is a great dish to make ahead. Have it ready in the baking dish, covered in your fridge. Add the orange juice right before baking.

If you're serving this dish with Greek or Indian food, you could put half a cinnamon stick in with the boiling water. This infuses each grain with a light cinnamon flavor, but it isn't as overpowering as sprinkling it on.

My latest favorite thing to do with rice is something I saw at an Indian restaurant recently. Throw a few pinches of cumin seeds into the pot of boiling rice as it cooks. It's so simple to do and it really adds amazing flavor. It's totally compatible with the orangey taste of this dish.

Wild Rice with Spinach and Luscious Lemon Cream

SERVES 4–6

There's something exciting about wild rice by itself, not just a few grains floating in a pilaf. You may have noticed I have a thing about wild rice. I like the taste of it and the look truly is wild. This can be a main course or a beautiful side dish. It's got texture and tang and that's always good. Of course, you could use any whole grain or variety of rice you like.

2 cups (500 mL) cooked wild rice

1 carrot, cut into matchsticks

1 large stalk celery, strings removed, finely chopped, leaves included

2 green onions, finely chopped

3 Tbsp (45 mL) olive oil

2 Tbsp (30 mL) flour

½ cup (125 mL) lemon juice

1–2 cups (250–500 mL) unsweetened soy milk

1 Tbsp (15 mL) lemon rind, finely grated

pinch of saffron

1 tsp (5 mL) onion powder

½ cup (125 mL) sunflower seeds, shelled

1 cup (250 mL) cherry or grape tomatoes

3 cups (750 mL) raw spinach leaves, washed and stemmed

one lemon, cut into circles

salt and pepper to taste

Preheat oven to 350°F (180°C).

Combine the wild rice, carrots, celery, green onions and toss in 1 Tbsp (15 mL) of olive oil. Pop this into the oven while preparing the other ingredients.

LEMON CREAM

In a saucepan, add the remaining olive oil and flour. Whisk constantly over medium heat. Add a bit of the lemon juice and whisk it in. Continue to add the lemon juice, and then the soy milk, whisking all the while. Whisk in the grated lemon rind, saffron and onion powder. Turn the heat to low and continue to simmer until you're ready to use it.

Remove the wild rice from the oven. Add the sunflower seeds, tomatoes and spinach leaves and toss them in. Put it in the oven only to warm it up, not to cook the celery or carrots completely—they should have some crunch. Season the dish with salt and pepper.

The lemon cream should be smooth and the consistency of heavy cream. Pour it over the top of the rice mixture and garnish it with the lemon slices.

Lemon juice in hot water makes a great cleansing antibacterial solution for gargling when you have a sore throat. Or do the traditional thing—a good shot of lemon in tea, when needed or desired.

A lemon tree bears fruit all year long. It can produce 500–2,000 lb of lemons.

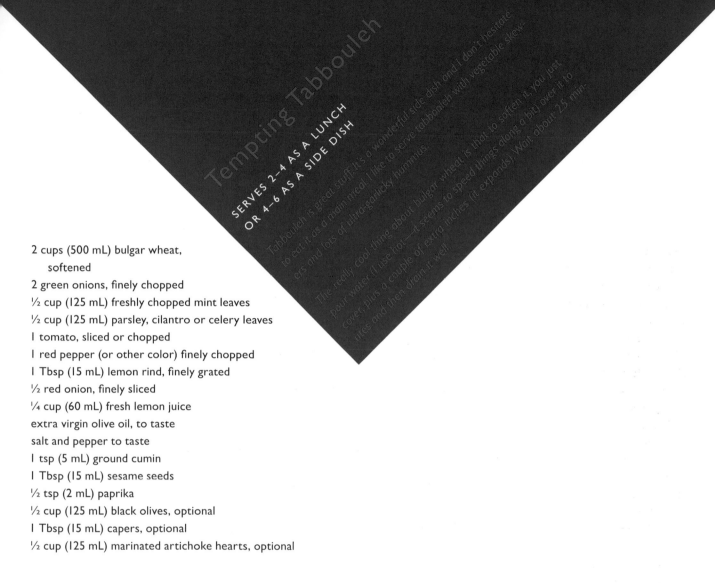

Tempting Tabbouleh

SERVES 2–4 AS A LUNCH OR 4–6 AS A SIDE DISH

Tabbouleh is great stuff. It's a wonderful side dish and I don't hesitate to eat it as a main meal. I like to serve tabbouleh with vegetable skewers and lots of ultra-garlicky hummus.

The really cool thing about bulgar wheat is that to soften it, you just pour water (I use hot—it seems to speed things along a bit) over it to cover, plus a couple of extra inches (it expands). Wait about 25 minutes and then drain it well.

2 cups (500 mL) bulgar wheat, softened
2 green onions, finely chopped
½ cup (125 mL) freshly chopped mint leaves
½ cup (125 mL) parsley, cilantro or celery leaves
1 tomato, sliced or chopped
1 red pepper (or other color) finely chopped
1 Tbsp (15 mL) lemon rind, finely grated
½ red onion, finely sliced
¼ cup (60 mL) fresh lemon juice
extra virgin olive oil, to taste
salt and pepper to taste
1 tsp (5 mL) ground cumin
1 Tbsp (15 mL) sesame seeds
½ tsp (2 mL) paprika
½ cup (125 mL) black olives, optional
1 Tbsp (15 mL) capers, optional
½ cup (125 mL) marinated artichoke hearts, optional

Take the drained bulgar wheat and add the other ingredients in with it. Traditionally, this can have a significant amount of oil in it. I suggest if you're using oil, add it last, 1 Tbsp (15 mL) at a time, then taste it. Or you could serve the oil at the table so that those who want it will drizzle it on top. However, if you add lots of great flavors you don't need any oil. The lemon is the key—taste and season. Arrange it on a plate and sprinkle it with sesame seeds and paprika.

Tabbouleh originated in Lebanon, where it is often spiced with allspice or a bit of cinnamon. It's also often served there by filling firm romaine lettuce leaves with the bulgar mixture.

You can make this recipe with other grains. Barley is truly delicious as a replacement. Quinoa's great for this too.

Colorful Black Thai Rice

SERVES 6–8 AS A MEAL

Cook this rice in the usual way: 2 cups (500 mL) of water to 1 cup (250 mL) of rice, but rinse the living daylights out of it first. Endless amounts of purple stuff will keep coming out of it. Rinse it well until the water runs almost clear.

2 cups (500 mL) cooked Black
   Thai rice
½ cup (125 mL) red pepper, diced
½ cup (125 mL) green pepper, diced
½ cup (125 mL) red onion, sliced
½ cup (125 mL) onion, finely chopped
½ cup (125 mL) cilantro, finely chopped
½ cup (125 mL) parsley, finely chopped
½ cup (125 mL) carrots, grated
rind of one orange, finely grated
rind of one lime, finely grated
½ cup (125 mL) lime juice
1 tsp (5 mL) toasted sesame oil
2 Tbsp (30 mL) extra virgin olive oil
salt and pepper to taste

You can simply combine the above ingredients and serve it at room temperature. If you prefer to serve it hot, here's an exciting way to do it:

Preheat oven to 400°F (200°C). Buy a frozen, packaged banana leaf (large grocery stores often have them). You won't believe the size of this leaf! Thaw it, take it out, put the rice mixture inside and wrap the leaf around it. Then, wrap the entire thing in foil on a baking sheet and bake it for a good 35 minutes.

About 5 minutes before serving, remove the foil so the leaf can crisp up a bit. The rice should be hot all the way through. Put the leaf-wrapped rice on a large platter and serve by placing it in the center of the table and unwrapping it or cutting through the banana leaf. It's very impressive and fun. The amazing fragrance of the rice will waft out, which will drive everyone wild! It's a great conversation starter for dinner parties.

Another beautiful way to serve rice in a banana leaf is to chop up a bunch of pineapple, mango and other tropical delights to add to the rice. Season it and bake it in the banana leaf, but then let it cool naturally. Eat it outside, under a palm tree if you're lucky enough to have one.

Colorful Black Thai Rice

You could probably find a way to turn almost every recipe in this book into a main course. I had a friend in high school whose mom used to make a big fruit salad for dinner! This might not have struck me as strange had we been in some hot or tropical place, but we weren't. It illustrates the point though: the rules are yours to make.

With V Cuisine, any meal can be a main course, a side dish or a snack—I chose these particular dishes to be main courses here, as a suggestion for you. A person who isn't a vegetarian might use most of the dishes presented here as side dishes or to do one for a main course one night a week.

You can determine if you want these to be main courses by your lifestyle. I serve the Superior Spring Rolls (page 139) for a main course for my family. I also serve them as party fare quite often. I even serve nachos as a main dish sometimes. I figure, the way I make it with a lot of beans and veggies—it's nutritious enough to do that. It's also easy to make and fun to eat. I make a lot of one pot dishes. There are so many ingredients in many of those that you can't go wrong.

I know people who eat soup twice a year and for them, that's enough. I could live on soup and be content on that forever, even if it's hot out. So for me, any soup could be a main course. But some people only eat a tiny bit as an appetizer now and then. It's all about having what you like and what you're in the mood for at the time.

I love the versatility of V Cuisine meals. I hope that you try some of these meals and enjoy them as much as I do. I know they'll give you lots of energy. I hope they get you excited about creating your own menus and make you passionate about food in general.

MODERN MAINS

Special Rapini Paella

I threw this odd dish together from a few refrigerator ingredients due to a hungry family hovering. As with all things new, some loved it more than others. Everybody ate it, if that counts for anything, although one picked out the peppers.

1 large onion, finely diced

2 garlic cloves, finely minced

3–4 Tbsp (45–60 mL) olive oil

1 full bunch of rapini, finely chopped

1 red pepper, finely chopped

3 cups (750 mL) cooked rice (½ brown, ½ basmati)

salt and pepper to taste

soy sauce to taste

Put the onion, garlic and oil into a hot pan. Stir constantly and cook until the onion is translucent. Add a bit of water if it starts to stick before it's cooked. Next, add the rapini and cook it down for about 3–5 minutes, stirring constantly. Then add the pepper and continue to cook for a couple of minutes more. Turn the heat to medium-low and add the rice, seasoning and soy sauce. Cook until it's hot and serve it immediately. This would be delicious with a green salad with a really tangy dressing, like Citrus-Hit Dressing (page 49) or any fruity vinaigrette.

This is a decadent-tasting meal, but you could certainly reduce the oil if you want to. You can put 1 Tbsp (15 mL) olive oil, with a bit of water, wine or whatever to cook down the veggies. It'll still be rich and delicious. Or you can always leave it out completely.

Since rapini is somewhat bitter, it's just becoming popular in North America. The Chinese (who call it choy sum) and the Italians use rapini frequently.

If you want the light bitterness of the rapini mellowed, simply blanch it in boiling water for one or two minutes.

An easy and delicious way to cook rapini is to sauté it in a little olive oil and a lot of garlic, then give it a good shot of fresh lemon when done.

There are so many great chili recipes out there. I hope this turns out to be one of your faves. Chili is one dish where you can make it vegetarian and it's just as exciting as the meat kind. The key to fabulous chili is in the simmering, the fresh ingredients, the sauce, the spicing and the combination of all of it. You'll love the smell of this wafting through the house! It's healthy, it tastes great and it's perfect to cook on the stove or overnight in a slow cooker. Try some for your next party.

Put the olive oil or 1 cup (250 mL) of water into a pot and heat it to high. Add the onions and garlic and any hot peppers you'd like to add, stirring constantly. When the onions become translucent, add the pepper, mushrooms and tomatoes. Cook this on medium until most of the liquid is gone. Add more water if there's very little liquid. Add the tomato sauce and the spices. Add the beans and chickpeas and turn the heat down to medium-low, just enough to keep the chili bubbling mellowly. Stir frequently to make sure it doesn't stick at all.

Taste and season the chili with hot sauce or cayenne pepper and/or black pepper and salt if desired. In my opinion, the longer this cooks, the better it gets. As the flavors marry along the way, taste it and add more heat or other flavors you desire.

2 Tbsp (30 mL) olive oil
2 big onions, peeled and diced small
6 cloves garlic (or more, to taste), finely minced
jalapeño peppers (or other hot peppers), chopped (optional)
1 green pepper, chopped
1 cup (250 mL) mushrooms, finely sliced
2 fresh tomatoes, chopped and/or 1 cup (250 mL) plum tomatoes, chopped
3 cups (750 mL) tomato sauce
1 tsp (5 mL) ground cumin
1 tsp (5 mL) paprika
1 tsp (5 mL) chili powder
1 cup (250 mL) canned kidney beans
½ cup (125 mL) canned black beans
½ cup (125 mL) canned chickpeas
salt and pepper to taste
hot sauce or cayenne pepper to taste (optional)

In major chili cook-offs in the USA, no beans are allowed! Other than finely chopped incidental vegetables (like peppers and onions), it's just meat, sauce and spices.

The famous outlaw of the American West, Jesse James (1847–1882) would not rob a bank in McKinney, Texas because his favorite chili restaurant was in that town.

Chili can be eaten out of a bowl or as a condiment. It's great for putting over potatos, grains or anything you like. You could stuff a pita with it or make a filling for something exotic.

Hippy Dippy Vegetarian Extravaganza

SERVES 4

As much as the whole V Cuisine concept is all about breaking out of the peasant skirt mode, we have to pay homage to those who began the "health food" movement. I mean the ones who ate the plain bean sprouts, the watery tofu and the mashed yeast—the stuff that scares people. It must have been rough to be one of those pioneers. There were no cool vegan products in the regular grocery store then.

1 cup (250 mL) firm tofu

½ cup (125 ml) extra virgin olive oil

¼ cup (60 mL) soy or teriyaki sauce

4 tsp (20 mL) onion powder

4 tsp (20 mL) garlic powder

4 tsp (20 mL) lemon juice

3 cups (750 mL) brown rice

16 cloves garlic, finely minced

4 cups (1 L) veggies, finely cut

4 tsp (20 mL) ginger

4 cups (1L) fresh spinach, washed

2 cups (500 mL) Miso Gravy (page 164)

2 cups (500 mL) bean sprouts

4 small beets, cut into mini matchsticks

2 carrots, grated

2 avocados

2 cups (500 mL) sunflower seeds and
    toasted pecans

¼ cup (60 mL) sesame seeds

8 green onions, sliced lengthwise and
    cut into pieces

sea salt and freshly cracked pepper
    to taste

Start by cutting the tofu into small slices or cubes. Then mix together 2 Tbsp (15 mL) of the olive oil with the soy sauce, garlic, onion powders and lemon juice. Pour over the tofu to marinate.

Cook the brown rice, (see How to Cook Rice, page 214) cover and set aside. Put the remainder of the olive oil into a pan with the garlic over medium heat. Add the tofu and the marinade. Add the veggies and ginger and stir-fry for a couple of minutes, stirring constantly. Remove from the heat.

Lay down a bed of spinach in 4 plates or 4 large, wide bowls. Layer with the brown rice, the Miso Gravy, then the veggies and tofu. Then make the top a show stopper: pile up the sprouts, your beautiful beets and carrots, and don't forget the avocado! Slice it up finely and arrange it on the top or around the edge.

Then sprinkle with sunflower seeds, toasted whole pecans and sesame seeds. Poke the green onion pieces in, or sprinkle them on. This truly is an extravaganza.

Can you imagine how difficult (and how expensive) it was to eat healthy food in the '60s?! Most parts of North America, other than small ethnic pockets, never even heard of tofu or bean sprouts, let alone used them.

Most people like sunflower seeds. They are a simple item to keep on hand for sprinkling on any kind of dish, from salad to grains to . . . well, anything really. Sunflower seeds in their shells are amazingly popular as a snack food. They're great for dieters because it takes time to get them out of the shells (although there are some pros out there).

Half-and-Half Dinner Bowl

SERVES 4

If you're like me, and feel like pasta, but you know that you won't stop at one plate, or even two, this dish can really work. This is just one example of a deliciously hearty sauce, but you could use any one you like. This dish may be a little weird, but who cares if it works!

THE SAUCE HALF

2 Tbsp (30 mL) olive oil

1 large onion, finely chopped

2 cloves garlic, finely minced

½ large eggplant, peeled and diced

1 cup (250 mL) wine or vegetable broth

1 cup (250 mL) vegetarian ground "beef" or cooked lentils

2 cups (500 mL) tomato sauce

1 tsp (5 mL) oregano or basil

salt and pepper to taste

Heat up the olive oil in a pan and add the garlic and onion. Cook them on high, stirring constantly until the onions are translucent. Add the eggplant and continue to stir. Add the wine or broth and reduce the heat to medium. Stir it well and cook about 5 more minutes, then add all the other ingredients and cover it. Turn the heat to low and simmer it for at least another 30 minutes.

THE VEGETABLE HALF

6 cups of shredded, grated or finely cut hearty vegetables

Some options: You can peel a zucchini, creating long strips like fettuccine. You can do the same with carrots. You can actually roll them around a fork if they're thin enough. Super finely sliced broccoli stalk is wonderful. What I like to do is to buy a bag of coleslaw that has the shredded purple and green cabbage and carrots. Whatever your choice, dry it in a salad spinner or with paper towels, then simply put it on one half of the dish. Put the sauce on the other half. Then you can dip the vegetable forkful into the sauce, or combine them as you wish.

You could use a lightly cooked vegetable for the veg half, if you prefer. Some steamed broccoli, asparagus, artichokes, green beans, snow peas, etc. would be terrific.

Remember if you have kids, and they're little, they won't think of a different dish as being "abnormal." They're fun to feed because you'll have a very open-minded clientele.

One of the best ways to keep hunger under control (and eating) is to not let yourself get to the point of starving. This is hard if you're busy, but even if you pack a little healthy snack (a fruit, a handful of nuts), your body will have something to process. You'll lose weight and feel so much better.

Panko-Stuffed Portobello Caps

SERVES 4

These are fantastic any time, any season of the year. The impressive size of the Portobellos makes anything made with them great. They have that "meaty" quality that makes them so appealing and with a lot of flavors added—wow. I like to include these as part of my holiday meals, but you don't have to wait for a special occasion to enjoy these.

3 Tbsp (45 mL) olive oil

1 large onion, finely chopped

1 bulb garlic, finely chopped

2 stalks celery, finely chopped

2 cups (500 mL) parsley, finely chopped

1 red pepper, finely chopped

1 tsp (5 mL) oregano

2 tsp (10 mL) sage

two 9-oz (255-g) containers panko (Japanese breadcrumbs)

1 cup (250 mL) vegetable broth

4 huge Portobello mushroom caps

Preheat oven to 425°F (220°C).

Add the olive oil, onion, garlic, celery, parsley and red pepper to a pan. Cook on high, stirring constantly, until the onions are translucent and the vegetables are tender. Mix in the panko, oregano and sage, and toss it well. Add enough of the veggie broth so that it holds together somewhat—then fill your Portobello caps up with the mixture, pressing it in tightly. Bake until the tops are golden brown.

Portobello (or Portobella) mushrooms are just a bigger version of criminis.

I recommend making an entire extra pan of stuffing to go along with these. People will usually want more, and even if you don't use it all at once, just cover and refrigerate it—it will be great in the fridge for a couple of days.

Panko-Stuffed Portobello Caps

Vivacious Vegetable Kabobs

SERVES 6

In summer, I consider these to be a staple food. If you use cherry tomatoes and fabulous mushrooms, this may not be the most inexpensive dish, but then again, it may be if you're trying to lose weight. It sure beats any specialty weight-loss meal in price and it's more delicious and surprisingly filling. You can eat them as is, perhaps adding a bit of extra firm tofu if you want more protein, or a small serving of brown rice or quinoa.

VEGETABLE SKEWERS

6 small zucchinis

30 cherry tomatoes

30 crimini mushrooms

1 green pepper

1 red pepper

1 orange or yellow pepper

2 large onions (red or white)

any other vegetable you like that'll stay on a skewer

MARINADE

6 garlic cloves, finely minced

1 cup (250 mL) ketchup

2 Tbsp (30 mL) Dijon mustard (or other variety)

¾ cup (175 mL) soy sauce

1 Tbsp (15 mL) lemon or lime juice

1 Tbsp (15 mL) balsamic vinegar

1 tsp (5 mL) onion powder

1 tsp (5 mL) Italian seasoning or oregano

salt and pepper to taste

Wash the veggies and cut them into skewer-size chunks. Put the veggies in a large container, which the skewers will fit into when they're done.

Mix all of the marinade ingredients together in a separate bowl. (Or just throw it in with the veggies and toss it together. You can probably guess which I do!)

You can also add in whatever herbs and spices you like. Instead of the Italian seasoning or oregano, you may want to try a curry/ground cumin combo, or some hot sauce. Or instead of the ketchup, use a thick teriyaki sauce and season it with lots of ginger and a drizzle of sesame oil.

Dress your vegetables and let them sit at least half an hour (I prefer an hour) so that the flavors can blend and be absorbed. Bamboo skewers hold the veggies a bit better than the metal ones. Skewer the vegetables and then barbecue them on medium heat until they're hot through and cooked as you like. This usually takes about 15 minutes, turning a couple of times along the way.

If you prefer to bake them; do so for about 20–25 minutes at 400°F (200°C), turning once. Or you can put them under a hot (high) broiler for a couple of minutes per side, watching constantly.

How done is done? Well, I like these cooked through, with the edges either starting to wither or slightly charred. Some people like these just heated through, so anything goes. Barbecuing vegetables is less picky on the timing than cooking meat.

Some other veggies you may want to try are carrots or potato. (You may have to lightly precook them so they'll go on a skewer without splitting, but not be so soft that they fall off). Leeks are great but wash them well. Experiment with different things. My son loves celery on a skewer, with vats of hot sauce poured over it.

Instead of putting your marinade on before skewering the veggies, you could skewer them first, and then brush the marinade on. Then your hands won't be a mess. The reason I do it the other way is to really get the marinade everywhere on each piece of vegetable.

If you want a richer marinade, add some olive oil to it. If you don't like the idea of ketchup, you could use barbecue sauce, mustard or anything with about the same thickness to replace it.

Magnificent Mochi

SERVES 6

Mochi is a weird and wonderful substance made from brown rice. It's blended to break up the rice grains. Then you can flavor it in lots of different ways. What's really cool is that when it's heated, it kind of puffs and melts, sort of like cheese. Caution: it's EXACTLY like cheese in one way—you can burn your tongue off if you're not careful!

2 cups (500 mL) cooked brown rice
1 cup (250 mL) unsweetened soy milk
    or water, broth, wine, etc.
2 cloves garlic, finely minced
½ tsp (2 mL) of Italian seasoning
salt and pepper to taste
1 tsp (5 mL) onion powder
½ cup (125 mL) nutritional yeast
drizzle of soy sauce

Preheat oven to 450°F (230°C).

Blend the brown rice, soy milk and garlic with an upright blender, food processor or a hand blender. Process it until it's as smooth as you can get it, adding more liquid if necessary.

Add all the seasonings (including the nutritional yeast and soy sauce) and mix it well. Prepare a baking sheet, with or without a sheet of parchment, with a little bit of olive oil. Spread the entire surface of the pan with the mochi mixture and then bake it for about half an hour.

This stuff freezes perfectly and has an eternal amount of uses. If you prefer, don't cook it at all, simply freeze it for use later on. Or, my favorite method is to place little 1-inch blobs onto a pan, placed about 1 inch apart. Then bake them and broil simultaneously if possible, at about 450°F (230°C). It's done when you think it's done!

You can form mochi into any shape you want. You can bread it and bake it. You can grate it (when it's frozen or well set up) onto pizza or anything and bake or broil to melt it. Try it—it's wild! Who knew?

Try this with a lot of finely chopped up jalapeño peppers and extra nutritional yeast; it's delicious. It makes a great party tidbit.

Traditionally, the Japanese make mochi out of glutinous rice that's pounded and formed into various shapes. They don't bake it again. They also make sweets out of it.

Revitalizing Veggie Stew

SERVES 6

I had a cooking class to teach once and the weather had been miserable for what seemed like forever. I wanted to show everyone something a little different that would energize them through the horrid weather. These ugly weather spells happen a lot where I live so I often try to think up dishes to bring people to life. So I came up with this recipe. The class turned out to be a party—the dish was fun to make, and most important, it warmed us all up,

1 Tbsp (15 mL) olive oil

1 medium onion, chopped

3 cloves garlic, finely chopped

1 stalk celery, chopped

1 carrot, cut into rings

1 green pepper, chopped

1 potato, chopped

1 cup (250 mL) mushrooms, halved

1 cup (250 mL) flat-leaf parsley, finely chopped

1 cup (250 mL) cooked wheat berries

½ cup (125 mL) cherry tomatoes

1 tsp (5 mL) ground cumin

½ tsp (2 mL) curry powder

½ tsp (2 mL) oregano

½ tsp (2 mL) basil

1 Tbsp (15 mL) soy sauce

½ cup (125 mL) nutritional yeast

salt and pepper to taste

Put the olive oil, onion, garlic and celery into a large pot, and cook on high, stirring constantly until the onions are translucent. Add the carrots, green pepper, potato, mushrooms and parsley. Add enough water to cover them, put a lid on it and simmer it on medium. As the water begins to evaporate, and the mixture thickens, add in the other ingredients, stirring it occasionally. When it has a thick and lovely consistency, it's ready to serve.

Mulligan stew is a pot of whatever you have on hand. If you want to be cost-effective with food, it's good to have a couple of throw-together dishes a week to use up vegetables while they're fresh.

Any time that 2 or more foods are slowly boiled or simmered in a liquid, it can be classified as a stew, or a ragout. We tend to think of these as being thicker than a soup, as the slow simmering usually results in a thick dish.

Revitalizing Veggie Stew

The "F" Word: Fondue!

SERVES 4–6

Enjoy this new age twist on a retro fave. The wine really makes this recipe. If you don't do wine, get a bottle of the non-alcoholized kind. Failing that, try 3 Tbsp (45 mL) unsweetened apple juice and 1 Tbsp (15 mL) lemon juice to give a hint of the wine flavor.

"F" is also for fun! Hope you have lots with this recipe.

2 Tbsp (30 mL) olive oil
1 large onion, chopped
1 bulb garlic (about 10 cloves), chopped
2 cups (500 mL) unsweetened soy milk
1½ cups (375 mL) cooked brown rice
½ cup (125 mL) roasted red peppers
1 cup (250 mL) nutritional yeast
1 tsp (5 mL) tarragon
½ tsp (2 mL) oregano or sage
1 cup (250 mL) dry white wine
salt and freshly ground pepper to taste
¼ cup (60 mL) finely chopped basil leaves
an assortment of veggies (peppers, zucchini, carrots, broccoli, cauliflower, etc.) Cut into 1–1½ inch (2.5– 4 cm) pieces for poking onto the ends of fondue forks. It's great to have these ready, plated and assembled in advance.
cherry or grape tomatoes, whole mushrooms and a variety of crusty breads cut into small pieces for skewering

Add the olive oil, onion and garlic to a pan, cooking them on high and stirring them constantly. When the onions are translucent, add 1 cup (250 mL) of soy milk, turn the heat down to medium-low and continue to simmer until the soy milk is nearly gone. Remove the pan from the heat.

Mix the onion/garlic mixture, cooked brown rice and the remainder of the soy milk, roasted red peppers, nutritional yeast, tarragon and oregano or sage. Using a hand or upright blender, or a food processor, blend it until it's smooth. If you need additional liquid to do so you can add some of the wine, or additional soy milk.

Put the mixture in a fondue pot on medium-low (it should remain at a low simmer). Add salt and pepper and the remainder of the wine and mix well. Add the basil leaves at the end.

Dip your vegetables and breads into this rich, cheese-like mixture.

If you don't have a fondue pot (although they're very inexpensive now), you don't need it for this recipe. Unlike cheese or chocolate fondues, which have to stay melty, or oil fondues that need to be hot to cook meat, you can simply take it off the stove and serve it. It'll be great. If you need to heat it up periodically, so be it. I doubt that it'll last long enough for that to happen though.

You could also use one of those mini slow cookers if you have one, or any other small electric pot that can keep something warm. Obviously use caution and make sure that the cord can't be yanked, tripped on, etc. There are also fondue pots with a burner underneath, so no need for cords.

The Swiss invented fondue to use up hardened cheese. The word comes from the French verb fondre, which means to melt.

For kids, why not make homemade pretzels for dipping? Start with the veggies and work your way to the pretzels.

These have enough flavors going on that the carnivores will love 'em too. I find that most meat eaters are pretty open to vegetarian foods, as long as they taste great. I can certainly relate to that idea—I don't want anything bland either!

Preheat oven to 400°F (200°C).

Put the wheat (or rye) berries and brown rice into a bowl. Use a hand blender or food processor to process about ½ or more of the grains, until it reaches a hamburger-like consistency. If you find you need liquid to make your blender work, simply add some of the wet ingredients like soy sauce or ketchup etc. When it holds together firmly if you pinch it, set it aside.

Put the olive oil, zucchini, onions, celery, garlic, bell pepper and mushrooms in a pan over medium to high heat, stirring the vegetables constantly, until the onions are translucent and everything is starting to cook through. Remove mixture from the heat and add it to the burger mixture. Mix well, adding the parsley, green onions, oregano, basil, mustard, soy sauce and seasonings.

Form burgers that are 2–3 inches (5–8 cm) across and about ½–1 inch (1–2.5 cm) thick. Place them on a baking sheet covered with parchment paper and bake them until they're firm (about 10–15 minutes). Flip the burgers carefully and bake them on the other side for 5–10 minutes. They should be firm enough to hold together but you don't want them to dry out. Do this baking in the oven step, even if you intend to barbecue the burgers—otherwise they tend to fall apart. Or you could wrap them individually in foil to prevent that.

You can also do them under a hot broiler. Just watch them carefully so they don't burn, turning to cook both sides.

1 cup (250 mL) cooked wheat or rye berries (or other whole grain)
1 cup (250 mL) cooked brown rice
2 Tbsp (30 mL) olive oil
1 zucchini finely chopped
1 large onion, finely chopped
1 stalk celery, finely chopped
4 cloves garlic, finely chopped
1 bell pepper, finely chopped
1 cup (250 mL) mushrooms (brown preferably), finely chopped
½ cup (125 mL) finely chopped fresh parsley
2 green onions, finely chopped
1 tsp (5 mL) oregano
1 tsp (5 mL) basil or sage, tarragon, etc.
½ cup (125 mL) ketchup
2 Tbsp (30 mL) mustard
½ cup soy sauce
salt and pepper to taste
hot sauce (optional)
1 good whole grain baguette bread (optional)

To serve baby burgers: Cut the baguettes into rounds. Place the burgers on each. Top them generously with something special, such as Roasted Tomato Chutney (page 170). Eat them immediately. You can toast the bread first if desired.

Veggie burgers are a lot of fun. The key is keeping them moist, as grains, nuts and vegetarian ingredients tend to dry out. So use lots of bits of watery vegetables (mushrooms, zucchini, etc.) to keep their moisture.

Multi-Mexies

These have all the naughty taste you'd get from a high-fat, fast food burrito, but they won't clog your arteries or make you feel like you just ate cement. They're also wonderfully versatile because you can use them in a million different ways.

twelve 8-inch (20-cm) Spring Roll
   Wraps (or flour or corn tortillas)
extras: olives, nutritional yeast, nuts,
   mushrooms, hot peppers, green onions,
   finely grated lime rind, avocado or better
   yet, guacamole! These are just a few ideas
   to sprinkle into the wraps for added greatness.

TOPPING

1 onion, chopped
5 cloves garlic, chopped
½ red pepper, chopped
2 tsp (10 mL) olive oil
1½ cups of vegetarian baked beans
1 tsp (5 mL) ground cumin
1 tsp (5 mL) paprika
½ tsp (5 mL) chili powder
cayenne pepper or hot sauce to taste

Put the onion, garlic, red pepper and oil into a pan, and then cover them with water. Heat them to boiling, then cover and simmer it on medium-low until everything is very tender. If there's any liquid, drain it off; you can use it to cook something else in.

Add the other ingredients and then blend it with an upright or hand blender to a smooth consistency. Keep it warm on low heat just before serving. Add liquid as needed to maintain a nacho sauce consistency.

FILLING

4 cloves garlic, finely chopped

I large onion, finely chopped

I green pepper, finely chopped

I Tbsp (15 mL) olive oil

I cup (250 mL) vegetables, finely chopped
    (zucchini, eggplant, peppers, potato, carrot,
    green beans, tomatoes, mushrooms—anything!)

II-oz (312-g) package vegetarian ground "beef"

½ cup (125 mL) tomato paste

I tsp (5 mL) ground cumin

I tsp (5 mL) oregano

I tsp (5 mL) onion powder

½ cup (125 mL) parsley or cilantro, finely chopped

salt and pepper (and hot sauce) to taste

Preheat oven to 350°F (180°C).

Add the garlic, onion, green pepper, olive oil and whatever veggies you've chosen in a pan over medium heat. Add enough water to cover it. Cook it until all the veggies are softened, and then add the veg ground "beef," tomato paste and spices. Simmer, uncovered, until it's thickened. Right before serving this, stir in the parsley or cilantro, taste and season it.

Put your wrap on a flat surface and place the filling down the middle. Pour a little bit of the topping over the filling. If you're so inclined, throw a few extras on there. Begin wrapping it, tuck the ends in, then continue wrapping to the end. To keep it soft, wrap it in foil, and bake it for about 10 minutes, just to heat it up. The sauces should already be warm, so it won't take long.

When I do this, I make another hot version of the topping sauce. Sometimes I'll switch the baked beans for chickpeas. Then I add hot sauce or a variety of hot spices.

To choose tortilla wraps, read the labels. If you have an awesome grocery store that has a lot of natural products you might find some good ones there. Otherwise, you'll probably have to look at a natural foods store or make your own—this is, of course, if you aren't using the spring roll wrappers.

Superior Spring Rolls

These make a zingy appetizer to ignite any party or a wonderful and unique supper. As a meal, they're lovely served along with a light stir-fry of snow peas, baby carrots and water chestnuts. That sounded good, but I never do that (ha ha). I just make the spring rolls as a meal. There are lots of veggies in them and it makes any old night feel festive.

Preheat oven to 425°F (220°C).

In a large pot, put enough oil to cook down the garlic and onions until the onions are translucent, at about medium-low heat. When they're done, crumble in the package of veg ground "beef." Add a little water or soy as required so that the mixture doesn't stick. At this time, you can add the ginger and about half of the cabbage. Cook it a couple of minutes more and season it. Lightly mash the tofu and then add it to the mixture. When it's piping hot, remove it from the heat and add the remainder of the cabbage. Toss it in; the filling is ready to use.

Peel apart several of the spring roll wraps. Take a small scoop of the filling and place it in the center of a wrap. You'll have more surface area if you work on the diagonal, but wrap it up however you like. Make a line of the filling, tuck in the sides, and roll it up. Add a drop or two of water to the final corner to help secure it shut. You should have a nice, snug little wrap. Remember, they're delicious overstuffed, but they may fall apart, so try to keep a reasonable balance between the filling and the wrap.

Bake for about 5–7 minutes per side or until golden brown and crispy. You may want to turn them once, to crisp up both sides. I realize something like this doesn't have "sides" but to brown them up front and back is plenty.

Cut them in half and serve them with plum sauce, soy or any other Asian-style sauce you love. They're fantastic with garlic-chili sauce if you like hot and spicy!

1–2 Tbsp (15-30 mL) olive oil

3 cloves garlic, finely minced

1 medium onion, finely diced

11-oz (312-g) package of vegetarian ground "beef"

soy sauce to taste

1 Tbsp (15 mL) powdered ginger

½ large cabbage, finely shredded

1 cup (250 mL) "traditional" or firm tofu

salt to taste

optional: hot sauce or white pepper to taste

spring roll wraps (The ones I use have 24 to a package and are about 8 inches (20 cm) across.)

Strangely enough, plum sauce with some soy sauce drizzled over the top is pretty great. The killer sweetness of the plum is broken up by the intensely fermented saltiness of the soy.

You can fill these with anything. Have some leftovers from that stir-fry the night before? Throw that in, for sure. I like to just crush up some navy beans and add a crazy amount of chopped green onion—it's excellent!

For the sweeter set: fill the spring roll wrappers with fresh peaches or a peach pie filling and lightly bake. Dust with a barely-there flurry of powdered sugar.

Lightened-Up Moussaka

If you love savory Greek moussaka, you won't believe this lower fat, non-meat, non-dairy version. I taught this in a class once where two burly men (dragged there by their wives) watched skeptically. As the class went on, I realized they didn't plan on liking it. Then they had some. BOTH of them rushed up to me after the class saying how much they loved the dish and that they would both be making it. If it won their hearts, hopefully it'll win yours!

3–4 large potatoes, cooked (baked or boiled)

¼ cup (60 mL) olive oil

salt and pepper to taste

2 cups (500 mL) unsweetened soy milk

1 cup (250 mL) breadcrumbs (or fine cornmeal)

2 tsp (10 mL) dried oregano

1 tsp (5 mL) garlic powder

1 tsp (5 mL) onion powder

1 medium eggplant, cut into ¼ inch (6 mm) rounds

2 onions, chopped

5 cloves garlic, finely chopped

28-oz (796-mL) can tomato sauce

11-oz (312-g) package vegetarian ground "beef"

1 tsp (5 mL) cinnamon

½ cup (125 mL) flat-leaf parsley, finely chopped

fresh basil leaves, if available, finely chopped

½ large cauliflower, boiled or steamed until soft

2 Tbsp (30 mL) flour

Preheat oven to 400°F (200°C).

Slice the potatoes thinly and lay them out on a parchment covered baking sheet. Drizzle with olive oil and season with salt and pepper. Then sprinkle them with a bit of water. Bake them in the preheated oven for about half an hour, turning when the tops are brown.

Put 1 cup (250 mL) of soy milk into a medium bowl. In another bowl, combine the breadcrumbs, oregano, garlic and onion powders and salt and pepper. Dip the eggplant rounds into the soy milk, then coat them with the breading mixture. Bake or broil them using the same method as the potatoes, until they're golden. Set them aside.

Put 2 Tbsp (30 mL) of oil into a pan over high heat and sauté the onions until translucent. Add the garlic and sauté a few more minutes. Add the tomato sauce, veggie ground "beef," cinnamon and parsley. Simmer for a few minutes until the parsley is wilted and the flavors have combined nicely. Add the basil, a few pinches of dried oregano and salt and pepper to taste.

To create the cream sauce, purée the cauliflower with 1 cup of soy milk using a hand blender, blender or food processor. When smooth, set aside.

Heat 2 Tbsp (30 mL) of olive oil over high heat in a small saucepan. Add 2 Tbsp (30 mL) of flour, and the remaining soy milk in small amounts, whisking constantly until it reaches a creamy consistency. Whisk in the cauliflower mixture. Season with salt and pepper and simmer over low heat.

Then comes the fun part—the assembly! Grease a smallish lasagna pan with olive oil. Then put about ¼ cup (60 mL) of sauce at the bottom and about ½ cup (125 mL) of water in. Then add a potato layer, a sauce layer, then an eggplant layer. Repeat layers until your ingredients are used up. Last, pour your decadent cauliflower cream sauce over the entire thing.

Bake for about half an hour until all the flavors are combined and the top is firm to the touch. If you want to brown it lightly under the broiler, do so. Enjoy!

Sumptuous Tempeh Mushroom Stroganoff

SERVES 4

Mushrooms and tempeh are the perfect duo, and this dish is loaded with mushrooms. I like it with a ton of onions too. I'm not trying to white bean you to death, but it makes the greatest sauce. If you're bored with them, however, you can replace them with the same amount of Basic White Sauce (page 171).

2 Tbsp (30 mL) olive oil

1 large onion, chopped

3 cloves garlic, finely chopped

1 cup (250 mL) flat-leaf parsley, finely chopped

1 cup dry sherry

1 cup (250 mL) sliced mushrooms, any variety

7.9-oz (255-g) package tempeh, thawed, cut into small cubes or strips

1½ cups canned navy beans, rinsed, drained and puréed

1 Tbsp (15 mL) dark soy sauce or dark mushroom soy sauce

½ cup (60 mL) red wine

1 tsp (5 mL) tarragon

salt and pepper to taste

additional flat-leaf parsley to garnish

3 cups (750 mL) egg noodle–like pasta (wide, short and slightly twisted)

Heat the olive oil and onions in a pot on high heat, stirring constantly. When the onions are translucent, add the garlic, parsley and a bit of the sherry. Keep stirring it and cook for 2 minutes. Add the mushrooms and the remainder of the sherry. Cover and cook over low heat for about 5 minutes. Add the tempeh and cook for another 5 minutes. Uncover, add the remainder of the ingredients, and cook until the sauce reaches a gorgeous, thick saucy consistency.

Cook the noodles in a separate pot and drain well. Drizzle with olive oil and toss lightly. Serve with the sauce and garnish with parsley. Serve something colorful on the side—a cherry tomato salad perhaps. This dinner is regal and has huge flavor!

The original Beef Stroganoff was apparently invented for a cooking competition and was made with beef tenderloin, plenty of mushrooms and sour cream as the base. A chef working for Count Pavel Alexandrovich Stroganov (a famous Russian general) created it.

Tempeh is high in B vitamins. The white mold that results from the fermentation of tempeh inhibits the growth of some deadly bacteria, including Staphylococcus aureus (which can cause food poisoning).

Torteenies with Artichoke and Spinach Pesto

SERVES 6

I had been making paninis (pressed Italian sandwiches) for years—they're awesome. So I used tortillas instead of bread one day and the torteenie was born. Tortilla + Panini = Torteenie. Enjoy this as a summer supper, a sophisticated lunch or something fun to bring on a picnic.

6 tortilla wraps

1 large zucchini sliced lengthwise, about ¼-inch (6-mm) thick

several Portobello mushrooms, sliced

several red, green and yellow peppers, cut in half and flattened

several asparagus spears, woody ends broken off

2 red onions, sliced into rounds about ¼-inch (6-mm) thick

VEGETABLE MARINADE

½ cup (125 mL) olive oil

¼ cup (60 mL) lemon juice or balsamic vinegar

¼ cup (60 mL) soy sauce

several cloves garlic, finely minced

1 green onion, finely minced

1 tsp (5 mL) oregano

1 tsp (5 mL) basil

1 tsp (5 mL) red pepper flakes (optional)

Mix together marinade and set aside. Combine the chopped vegetables and the marinade and let sit for 30 minutes. To cook the vegetables, simply place them on a hot grill, until they're done to your liking. If you don't have a grill available, simply put them under a broiler, watching them constantly and turning them when done on top.

PESTO

5 cloves garlic, chopped
2 green onions, chopped
3 Tbsp (45 mL) olive oil
¼ cup (60 mL) fresh lemon juice
1 cup (250 mL) flat-leaf parsley, coarsely chopped
2 cups (500 mL) artichokes, marinated or not
½ cup (125 mL) pine nuts or slivered almonds
5–6 cups (1.25–1.5 L) fresh spinach leaves, stemmed
several fresh basil leaves
salt and pepper to taste

In a food processor, add all the pesto ingredients and pulse until well-combined. It should be leafy, but somewhat spreadable. If you don't have a food processor, simply chop everything as finely as you possibly can, then mash it with a fork or pastry cutter to combine all the flavors and make it spreadable.

Take the tortilla wraps and spread some of the pesto all over one side. Then on one half, assemble the grilled vegetables. Fold over the tortilla wrap, then set it into the hot panini press or on the pan with the other pan on top. If half a tortilla is too large for your pan or panini press, cut it in half.

You just have to heat everything through and brown the tortilla slightly. Check the side that's cooking often if you're using the pan method. Flip it when it's heated through. It should take only a couple of minutes in the panini press and it will probably be ready to flip when defined grill marks appear.

To make torteenies you can cook them on a panini press or simply put a pan on medium-low. Then, put parchment on the bottom of the pan or a drizzle of olive oil, and press on the top with another pan.

The word panini is a diminutive of the word "pane," which means bread in Italian. The singular is panino. So technically, this would be a "torteeno."

Panini presses, which were an expensive specialty item a few years ago, are common now, much cheaper and a good thing to have. You can grill lots of things on them, and there are a lot of great models to choose from.

You can actually grill little raviolis (already boiled) in Panini presses—it's amazingly good. Just serve them with something to dip into on the side. I boil the raviolis lightly first.

Whether or not you're lucky enough to go to a real party every night, every night should feel like a party. You might wonder how decadent, rich, wild party food can possibly translate into vegan fare. Wonder no more! V Cuisine delivers fresh ideas about party food. People are excited about healthier food for socializing that still tastes sinful.

My concept of party food is three-fold. First, it has to taste great. Second, it has to be colorful and look beautiful. Third, and perhaps most importantly, it has to be easy to hold and eat. Kids and snackers alike know the importance of finger food (they tend to be multi-taskers too!). I want you to be able to celebrate life with amazing food that fulfills all this criteria. And it won't make you feel bloated or horrid the next day.

Best of all, there's nothing too difficult here. Unlike seafood, or complex baking, cooking times aren't that crucial unless stated. The components of each can be made in various ways and flavored the way you want. You can simply add other herbs and spices and flip it into something else.

So Party On! Whether it's at a big city gala, or your own kitchen table, live it up today and always.

LIFE OF THE PARTY FARE

Pretty Party Pâté

SERVES 4–6

This is a funky, kind of retro '60s style pâté that's cool to serve at a party with lots of chips and dips. Garnish it all around with lots of green stuff, maybe some celery leaves and plenty of parsley. Dot with cherry tomatoes to really add some festivity.

2 cups (500 mL) canned navy beans

1 Tbsp (15 mL) extra virgin olive oil

1 Tbsp (15 mL) lemon or lime juice

1 mini sweet pickle (baby gherkin), chopped tiny

1 dill pickle, chopped tiny

1 stalk celery, chopped tiny

1 green onion, chopped tiny

½ tsp (2 mL) garlic powder

½ tsp (2 mL) onion powder

dash of hot sauce or horseradish

½ tsp (2 mL) mild curry powder

½ tsp (2 mL) celery seed or celery powder

salt and pepper to taste, if desired

½ tsp (2 mL) paprika (for sprinkling on top)

Blend the navy beans, olive oil and lemon or lime juice in a food processor until the mixture is smooth. You can use a blender, but only if you can do it without adding more liquid. That would mellow the flavor out too much and this has to rock! Transfer the mixture into another bowl, add in all the other ingredients and stir it well.

Next, find something to use as a mold; a terrine pan or the right-sized bowl. Line the mold with plastic wrap and fill it up with the mixture, pressing it in with a spoon or spatula so there are no gaps. Cover it with plastic wrap and place it in the refrigerator for a couple of hours to set and chill it. It will be easy to take out because of the plastic wrap. Turn it out on a serving platter by pulling it out with the plastic wrap. Peel off the wrap and garnish it as you like.

This would make a savory sandwich spread. To make those sandwiches even more fun, toast the bread, spread with the pâté and add an obscene amount of watercress.

Due to the fact that pâtés are usually baked in terrine pans, the terms "pâté" and "terrine" tend to be used interchangeably.

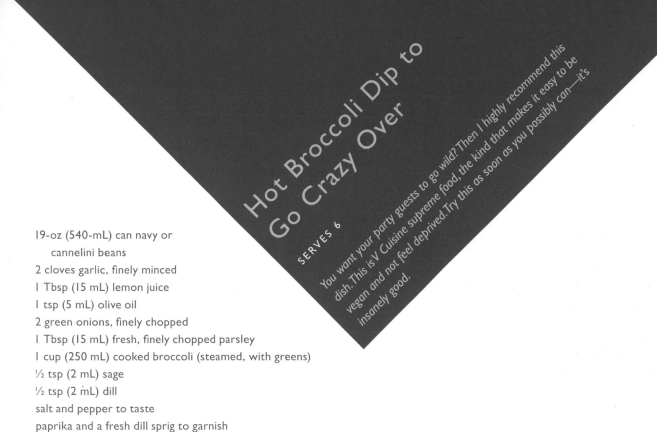

Hot Broccoli Dip to Go Crazy Over

SERVES 6

You want your party guests to go wild? Then I highly recommend this dish. This is V Cuisine supreme food, the kind that makes it easy to be vegan and not feel deprived. Try this as soon as you possibly can—it's insanely good.

19-oz (540-mL) can navy or
   cannelini beans
2 cloves garlic, finely minced
1 Tbsp (15 mL) lemon juice
1 tsp (5 mL) olive oil
2 green onions, finely chopped
1 Tbsp (15 mL) fresh, finely chopped parsley
1 cup (250 mL) cooked broccoli (steamed, with greens)
½ tsp (2 mL) sage
½ tsp (2 mL) dill
salt and pepper to taste
paprika and a fresh dill sprig to garnish

Preheat oven to 400°F (200°C).

Blend the beans, garlic, lemon juice and olive oil in a food processor until smooth. Or you could mash them well with a fork. Then add the green onion, parsley, broccoli, sage, dill and salt and pepper. Oil a small baking dish and put the mixture into it, smoothing the top with a spoon, so it looks good. Sprinkle the top with paprika and bake until it's good and hot (about 20 minutes). Stick a dill sprig in the top and serve.

Serve this with tortilla chips, veggies or little breads. It's to die for with cherry tomatoes too.

This actually makes a great condiment. It accompanies whole grains perfectly. Or serve it with a warm spinach salad or any steamed greens. Of course, it's perfect with broccoli.

This dip is brilliant served cold. Hollow out a tomato and fill it with this dip, and serve it with multi-grain toast points on a gorgeous plate for each person at a luncheon. Superb.

Unexpected Dip

SERVES 8–10

When you're having company at the last minute, or a casual summer supper, this is a fun thing to make. It has a ton of flavors, and it's fresh and uplifting. It's a little reminiscent of those Mexican-style layered dips that were popular in the late '70s, without the heavy sour cream and cheddar cheese.

2 cups (500 mL) black beans
2 Tbsp extra virgin olive oil
2 perfectly ripe avocados
2 ripe tomatoes, chopped
2 small jalapeño peppers, seeded and chopped
1 cup (250 mL) almonds, in slivers
1 large carrot, cut into fine matchsticks or grated
2 green onions, finely chopped
salt and pepper to taste
fresh lemon or lime juice
tortilla chips to serve with

Rinse the black beans well and mash them with a fork, coarsely. Add the olive oil and continue to mash them to a paste-like consistency. Lightly season with salt. Take a wide, shallow bowl or a pie plate and layer the beans at the bottom. Next, peel and pit the avocados and coarsely mash them. Lightly salt and drizzle the avocados with the lemon or lime juice. Layer over the beans.

Toss the chopped tomatoes and jalapeños together. Lightly salt and drizzle them with lemon or lime juice. Add that layer atop the avocado. Next, make a layer with the almonds. Then take the grated carrot and make a circle on top of the almonds, all around the edge. Sprinkle on the crisp green onions and serve it with tortilla chips. The blue corn tortilla chips or the naturally colored red ones would be fantastic.

Bake tortilla chips in the oven at about 350°F (180°C) for about 5 minutes, just to warm them up—they'll taste like the freshly made ones.

Other flavor-boosters for this dish: ground cumin, fresh, chopped cilantro or hot sauce to taste if desired.

This dish has fantastic protein with the almonds and beans. And with all those fresh vegetables in it—you can't help but feel *alive*.

Ever see the candy-coated almonds at Italian weddings? They're usually wrapped in netting and given as favors. Five almonds are for five wishes for the couple: happiness, health, wealth, fertility and long life.

Stuffed Mushroom Caps with Zap

SERVES 7–10

I prefer crimini (brown) mushrooms, but you can use what you like. I used to be a purist about reusing the stems in the recipe by making them part of the filling, but now I toss them if I don't like the looks of them. If they're super decent (rare), I may reuse them in a veg stock the next day.

about 20 mushrooms,
    stems removed
2 cups (500 mL) cooked brown rice
½ cup (125 mL) chopped kalamata,
    stuffed green or other olives
¼ cup (60 mL) chopped green onion
¼ cup (60 mL) chopped fresh parsley or cilantro
1 tsp (5 mL) basil
1 tsp (5 mL) oregano
1 tsp (5 mL) minced garlic or garlic powder
1 tsp (5 mL) onion powder
soy sauce to taste
salt and pepper to taste

Preheat oven to 400°F (200°F).

Process the rice in a food processor, or blend it with a hand blender, a few good pulses to combine it and break up the rice grains. Then add the other ingredients and mix it well. It should stick together if you squeeze some of the mixture. You can add more flavors (such as mustard or hot sauce) if you like.

Fill the caps; it's okay to overstuff in this case. Enjoy this moment because usually overstuffing results in a problem, but not this time. If you have more filling than mushrooms, you can bake it in little blobs for a different kind of little snack.

Bake for about 20 minutes. You want the filling to be golden brown and firm. Or bake them for 10 minutes and then turn the broiler on high for a minute or two, watching them continuously so they don't burn.

Serve 4 on a bed of spinach as an appetizer, or a couple alongside a meal of finger foods, as a side dish with practically anything, or as a snack. They can be as elegant or as casual as you wish.

Crimini mushrooms—yum. They're a richer-flavored, darker mushroom than the typical white kind. They are also far more dense, which gives them their "meaty" texture.

A Portobello mushroom has more potassium than a banana.

You can make these and put them on the barbecue for added smoky flavor. Just bake or lightly broil them in the oven first so that they're firm enough to hold together, or golden on top. Then just heat them up on the barbecue for a real taste sensation.

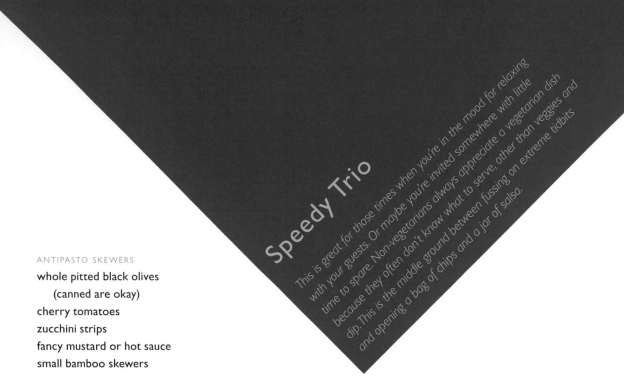

Speedy Trio

This is great for those times when you're in the mood for relaxing with your guests. Or maybe you're invited somewhere with little time to spare. Non-vegetarians always appreciate a vegetarian dish because they often don't know what to serve, other than veggies and dip. This is the middle ground between fussing on extreme tidbits and opening a bag of chips and a jar of salsa.

ANTIPASTO SKEWERS

whole pitted black olives
    (canned are okay)
cherry tomatoes
zucchini strips
fancy mustard or hot sauce
small bamboo skewers

Take a skewer and "weave" a zucchini strip between alternating cherry tomatoes and olives. In other words, skewer the zucchini strip near the end, but not so close that it will split to the end and fall off. Then put a cherry tomato, then the next part of the zucchini strip, then an olive, next part of the strip, tomato, strip, olive, strip, tomato, etc. Continue to the end.

You could marinate these, but then it becomes a drippy affair and you'd need plates, napkins, etc. I think I'd give them a quick dusting with fine salt and pepper, then dot with the hot sauce and/or mustard and serve.

STUFFED OLIVES

large pitted green olives (without pimentos)
whole cashews or almonds

Stuff as many green olives with the cashews and/or almonds as you wish to serve. This is a bit of a surprise instead of the usual pimentos. Place them on a funky plate or bowl with a colorful napkin. You can also do this with whole garlic cloves for the more adventurous.

CUCUMBER/BEAN/TOMATO BITES

large fava beans (canned are fine)
cucumber strips
sun-dried tomatoes, softened
orange rind, finely grated
toothpicks

If the sun-dried tomatoes aren't soft (the oil or other marinated kind) immerse them in a bit of hot water, oil or other liquid you like. When they're soft, drain it off and dry them.

Cut the cucumber in half lengthwise, scoop out the seeds with a spoon, then peel in wide paper-thin strips. The swiveling head peelers do a good job of this. Take a fava bean and a sun-dried tomato, wrap both with one cucumber strip (or a portion of it—just so they're wrapped) and put them on a toothpick. Garnish each with a pinch of grated orange rind (or grated lemon or lime rind if you prefer). These look fantastic and taste deliciously unusual.

This is the perfect food project type of prep for kids. If you have all of the ingredients ready to go, you could make one, and then the kids could take it from there. To let them reap the reward of how much people will enjoy their creations, why not let them serve too? One less thing you have to do.

Black Bean Tomato Poppers

SERVES 10 (BASED ON 3 EACH)

This may sound like the pickiest little recipe you've ever encountered! I think it's worth the effort (but then, I can be a bit of a detail freak). Its eye appeal is major and people tend to light up when they see these bite-sized morsels.

1 cup (250 mL) canned black
　　beans, mashed or blended smooth
1 clove garlic, finely minced
1 green onion, finely chopped
¼ cup parsley, finely chopped
1 stalk celery, ultra-finely chopped
drizzle of extra virgin olive oil (optional)
drizzle of lemon juice
salt and pepper to taste
pinch ground cumin
20–30 cherry tomatoes (depending on
　　size—it varies greatly)

To stuff the cherry tomatoes, you don't hollow them out as thoroughly as you would a large tomato. And you don't have to cut off the teeny little top to make a lid in the same way. Simply cut the top off as best you can. Take out a bit of the wet part and seeds of the tomato with a tiny spoon or a fine olive fork. Stuff it with the filling and replace the sliced-off top. Or sprinkle it with seeds, parsley or anything you think looks festive; this can be instead of the little tomato hat if you like.

You can serve this on a bed of greens or on a plate covered in coarse salt (very modern and attractive). It also keeps them from rolling around! You might even need to slice off a tiny bit of the tomato on the bottom to make it sit flat.

Try this at your next party, or when you need an appetizer that's a little different and exciting. And if the black bean thing doesn't do it for you, then stuff with hummus or another dip you like.

Cumin is second only to black pepper in the spice realm.

Parsley makes great "bouquets." Just have plain, simple modern glasses or small vases and put some bunches of parsley in them, in water. It's great to use edible decorations.

You could put a little grated lemon rind sprinkled on top of each tomato popper, if you want to get fancy.

Zucchini-Wrapped Quinoa (page 156), Black Bean Tomato Poppers (page 152), Wild Rounds (page 154)

Wild Rounds

You thought I was colorful before? There's nothing like beets for some good, fluorescent color. You might want to wear gloves and an apron for this (or a beekeeper's outfit!) unless you want to be beet-colored too. I created these because I specifically wanted something crazily colored for a party.

2 long English cucumbers
1 cup (250 mL) beet juice
1 cup (250 mL) cooked carrots
1 cup (250 mL) canned navy beans
1 Tbsp (15 mL) olive oil
½ cup (125 mL) unsweetened soy milk
1 tsp (5 mL) onion powder
1 clove garlic, chopped
½ tsp (2 mL) turmeric
½ tsp (2 mL) ground cumin
salt and pepper to taste
2 green onions, finely chopped
¼ cup (60 mL) toasted sesame seeds
¼ cup (60 mL) poppy seeds

Cut the cucumbers in half (not lengthwise). Use a butter knife to remove the seeds, so that you have 4 hollow cucumber tubes. Soak them in the beet juice, turning, until they're saturated with color. Set aside on paper towels to drain.

Blend together the carrots, navy beans, olive oil, soy milk, onion powder, garlic, turmeric, ground cumin and salt and pepper with a hand blender. Then add in the chopped green onions, saving a little bit for a garnish.

Using a butter knife, fill the tubes with the mixture. If you're not serving this immediately, wrap them well with plastic wrap and refrigerate.

To serve, slice the cucumbers into ½-inch (1-cm) thick rounds, adding green onions on the top. Dip some of the rounds in sesame seeds and some in poppy seeds for a bit of a showstopper.

Beet juice is terrific for coloring things. A couple of drops in something won't affect the taste greatly. I like to color savory things as well as sweet—experiment if you like wild colors. It's fun. Try making some pink potatoes or cauliflower for a little princess!

Turmeric is a significant ingredient in many curry powders. It also colors most commercial mustard. In Ayervedic medicine, it's considered to have health benefits. People in India use it to treat cuts and burns. Some Asian countries use it as a supplement, and to treat digestive problems. Turmeric is related to the ginger plant and is used to make a tea in Okinawa, Japan.

Barley Balls

When people are partying, they really appreciate having some healthy munchables. It's so much more fun to be able to eat and not be sorry the next day. These little balls are fun, uncomplicated finger food.

2 cups (500 mL) cooked barley
2 cloves garlic, finely minced
1 green onion, finely chopped
1 tsp (5 mL) onion powder
1 tsp (5 mL) Dijon mustard
1 tsp (5 mL) light miso
1 tsp (5 mL) soy sauce
1 tsp (5 mL) ground cumin
1 Tbsp (15 mL) wheat germ
red pepper flakes to taste (optional)
salt and pepper to taste

Preheat oven to 425°F (220°F).

Stir all of the ingredients together. Form into 1-inch (2.5-cm) balls and place them on a lightly oiled baking sheet, or a sheet covered with parchment. Bake them for about 25 minutes, turning them once. They should be lightly golden.

Serve plain or with a dipping sauce. Miso Gravy (page 164) with green onion added would be great. So would cocktail sauce or a simple teriyaki sauce out of a bottle, with added green onion.

These also make a great appetizer. Try serving 5 or 6 of these on a bed of sautéed greens or on a pool of red pepper sauce, for each person.

You could omit the ground cumin and add 1 Tbsp (15 mL) of freshly chopped dill. Excellent!

Barley was one of the earliest cereal crops, used by the ancient Greeks, Romans, Chinese and Egyptians.

Zucchini-Wrapped Quinoa

SERVES 8–12

These make gorgeous little party snacks. For those who haven't tried quinoa, it's a great new sensation. It's an ancient grain that's becoming very popular. These are colorful, tasty and low in fat. Enjoy!

1 medium zucchini, in thin strips
2 cups (500 mL) quinoa (cooked)
1 tsp (5 mL) ground cumin
1 tsp (5 mL) garlic powder
2 green onions, finely chopped
drizzle of olive oil
1 carrot, grated
¾ cup silken tofu (or any vegetable or bean purée)
salt and pepper to taste
toothpicks (to hold together) (optional)

Put the quinoa in a bowl with all the ingredients except the zucchini, and season. If there are other flavors you'd like to add, experiment. Dill is wonderful, or perhaps you'd like a dash of teriyaki or hot sauce. As far as I'm concerned, you can never go wrong with mustard.

Use a peeler to make fine strips of zucchini. If possible, use an organic zucchini and don't peel it—then your strips will have a beautiful, dark green edge. Fill each strip with a spoonful of the mixture, wrap it up and skewer it with a toothpick. I've served them upright (the strips rolled around with the hole at the top, then filled, or on their sides).

Serve them as is, or heat them up gently in a warm oven, just before serving.

These are truly beautiful!

The quinoa should be fluffy, with little round "sprouts" on each. The taste is terrific—kind of chewy and nutty. What has more protein and calcium than a quart of milk? A cup of quinoa!

When you want a whole grain, but don't feel like cooking for hours, go for quinoa—it cooks up quickly and can be a great bed for saucy things. Or make a gorgeous pilaf out of it.

Tofu might seem like an oddball ingredient here. But it makes the perfect binder and flavor picker-upper.

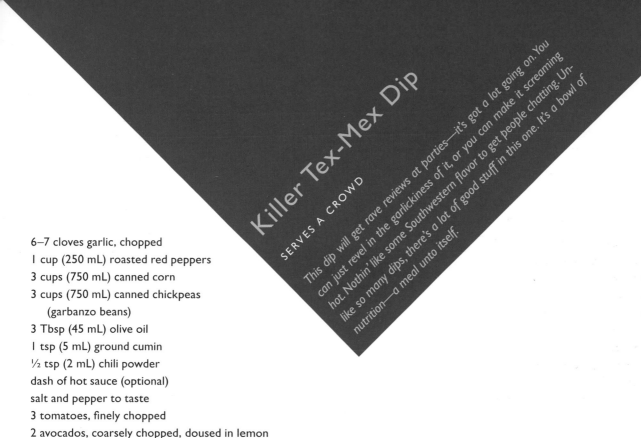

Killer Tex-Mex Dip

SERVES A CROWD

This dip will get rave reviews at parties—it's got a lot going on. You can just revel in the garlickiness of it, or you can make it screaming hot. Nothin' like some Southwestern flavor to get people chatting. Unlike so many dips, there's a lot of good stuff in this one. It's a bowl of nutrition—a meal unto itself.

6–7 cloves garlic, chopped

1 cup (250 mL) roasted red peppers

3 cups (750 mL) canned corn

3 cups (750 mL) canned chickpeas
   (garbanzo beans)

3 Tbsp (45 mL) olive oil

1 tsp (5 mL) ground cumin

½ tsp (2 mL) chili powder

dash of hot sauce (optional)

salt and pepper to taste

3 tomatoes, finely chopped

2 avocados, coarsely chopped, doused in lemon
   or other citrus juice

2 green peppers, finely chopped

1 cup (250 mL) cilantro, finely chopped

bag of tortilla chips

Preheat oven to 375°F (190°C).

Using a hand blender or food processor, coarsely blend the garlic, roasted red peppers, corn, chickpeas, 2 tsp (10 mL) olive oil, ground cumin, chili powder, hot sauce and salt and pepper. Mix in the remaining ingredients by hand, then put the mixture into a lightly oiled 9-inch (1.5-L) pie plate and bake it until it's heated through.

Place the tortilla chips on a baking sheet and cook them for about 5 minutes, just to heat them up and bring out the flavor.

Chickpeas are common in Mediterranean and Middle Eastern cooking. They have great nutrition and are completely delicious.

If you're cutting calories, look for the baked tortilla chips—you won't mind any difference when eating them with a tasty dip. Always read the labels. Some have a couple of simple ingredients (perfect) or some are just plain too awful to eat.

Party Polenta Squares

The magic of cornmeal strikes again—these are easy to make and fun to eat. Put any topping you like on them. Kids and adults alike really seem to love polenta and it's so versatile. You can form it into various shapes and flavor it any way you like. Serve this as an appetizer, party food or have several as a meal, alongside a big green salad.

3 cups (750 mL) cornmeal
I tsp (5 mL) garlic powder
I tsp (5 mL) onion powder
I tsp (5 mL) ground rosemary
I tsp (5 mL) thyme
I tsp (5 mL) marjoram
salt and pepper to taste

TOPPING

I Tbsp (15 mL) olive oil
I cup (250 mL) mushrooms, finely
    sliced
I onion, finely chopped
3 cloves garlic, finely minced
1½ cups (375 mL) canned or cooked
    lentils
2–3 fresh tomatoes, chopped
fresh herbs, finely chopped
salt and pepper to taste

Preheat oven to 425°F (220°C).

In a large pot, boil 6 cups (1.5 L) of water until it's at a full rolling boil. Add a few pinches of salt and the cornmeal. Turn the heat down to medium-low. Whisking constantly, cook until all the cornmeal has absorbed all of the water and it's thick and bubbly (usually about 5 minutes).

Combine the cornmeal with the seasonings and mix well.

Lightly oil a 13- x 9- inch (3.5 L) casserole pan and put the cornmeal into it. Spread it out evenly to the edges.

Wait until it sets up, about 10-15 minutes, then cut it into approx. 3 inch (8 cm) squares. Remove the squares and place them on a baking sheet covered in parchment. Bake in a 425°F (220°C) oven until the edges are golden and the squares are firm and hot.

FOR THE TOPPING

Cook the olive oil (or other liquid), mushrooms, onions and garlic over high heat, stirring constantly. When the onions are translucent, remove them from the heat and cool slightly. Coarsely mash the lentils and add them to the cooked mixture. Add the tomatoes and fresh herbs to the cooked mixture. Season it with pepper and salt.

Top each square with a generous helping of the delicious topping.

To make polenta croutons, cut the cornbread into tiny little cubes, about ½ inch (1 cm). Bake them the same way as the squares, making sure to separate them. Place them at least ½-inch (1 cm) apart on the baking pan. These are awesome for homemade soup, especially tomato-based ones.

Another good thing to do with polenta is just make a thin base with it and cover it with lots of carmelized onions (roasted in the oven). Call it an onion pie or tart—more great party food.

Super Sesame "Fries"

SERVES 4–6

These should definitely come with a warning. They're extremely addictive. The sesame seeds give better food value (loaded with calcium) than ordinary old fries, but you may want to eat a lot of them often. They're always a big hit at parties, served with a dip or with Miso Gravy. They're also super good with homemade barbecue sauce.

5–6 good-sized potatoes
olive oil to coat
salt to taste
about ⅓ cup (75 mL) sesame seeds

Preheat oven to 425°F (220°C).

Follow the French "Fried" Potatoes (page 88) in the Potato Oasis section. Then, liberally sprinkle the potatoes with the sesame seeds and bake them as normal, keeping an extra good eye on them so the seeds don't burn.

I really like to have a batch ready on a baking sheet in my fridge, covered. When I have a backyard barbecue in the summer and it's hours after the main meal but the party is still in full swing, I pop them into the oven. Everyone seems to perk up when these come around.

These make a nice dinner paired with a green salad and a small bowl of chili. You could even make the chili extra thick and spicy and make the "fries" really broad, thick homestyle ones and dip them.

Want to be truly decadent? Dip these babies into some gorgeously creamy guacamole!

Have you ever tried making paper thin potato slices and putting a beautiful herb between two? Then you bake your "potato chips" with this gorgeous leaf on the inside—it's super cool.

Hot Artichoke Dip

SERVES A CROWD

A friend of mine used to make a hot party dip with tuna fish, mayo and sour cream. It had a ton of garlic and onions and was oven-baked. Everyone loved this stuff. I wanted a vegan hot dip that was amazing too. This is it. It has all the same flavors going on as well as artichokes, one of the darlings of the vegetarian realm.

3 cups (750 mL) artichokes (canned
   or jarred—marinated are fine)
19-oz (540-mL) can white beans (navy,
   cannelini or white kidney)
1 tsp (5 mL) olive oil
1 tsp (5 mL) Dijon mustard
½ cup (125 mL) unsweetened soy milk
2 cloves garlic, finely minced
2 green onions, finely chopped
pinch of basil, oregano, sage or dill
salt and pepper to taste
tortilla chips (preferably the red or blue corn,
   but any will do)

Preheat oven to 425°F (220°C).

Combine the artichokes, beans, olive oil, Dijon mustard and soy milk. Blend with an upright or hand blender until you have a somewhat smooth mixture (it's okay to have a few chunks of artichoke—good even). Add the garlic, green onions and seasonings.

Lightly olive oil an 8-inch (1.2-L) pie plate and put the mixture in, spreading it evenly to the sides. Bake it until golden on the top and hot, usually about 20 minutes. You could pop the chips under foil and bake them for the last 5 minutes so they don't burn. Heating them up makes them crisp and delicious.

Serve the dip hot with chips, small breads or crackers, or as a condiment for almost anything.

An artichoke is the bulb of a flower from the thistle family.

You can really never have too much of a good thing. I've actually eaten this dip on artichokes, sprinkled with tons of fresh, finely chopped parsley.

Some sources say artichokes originated in Sicily. In medieval times, they were considered an aphrodisiac and women were forbidden to eat them!

Castroville, California is called the "Artichoke Capital of the World." Marilyn Monroe is said to have held the title of the first "Artichoke Queen" there in 1948.

Those Little Rice Balls

What's best about these is that they're finger food and that you can flavor them any way you like—an Asian spin is nice. These are always popular at a party.

3 cups (750 mL) cooked brown rice

1 onion finely chopped

2 cloves garlic, finely minced

1 Tbsp (15 mL) Dijon mustard

1 tsp (5 mL) Italian seasoning (or basil/oregano)

½ cup (125 mL) nutritional yeast

drizzle of olive oil

1 cup (250 mL) unsweetened soy milk or veggie broth

1 package (312 g) vegetarian ground "beef"

½ cup (125 mL) fresh, chopped parsley

Preheat oven to 425°F (220°C).

Add all the ingredients together except for the vegetarian ground "beef" and the parsley. Mix it well and then use an upright or hand blender to blend up about ¼ of the mixture. Add it to the rest and mix again. Add the vegetarian ground "beef" and parsley.

Form the mixture into little balls, about 1 inch (2.5 cm) each, and bake them until the outsides become firm and the balls are heated through, about 20 minutes. You might want to turn them once. You can also broil them on high, if you're willing to watch them the whole time, turning.

In Burma, the average person eats 500 lb of rice a year! That works out to about 1¼ lb per day.

Rice is not just a food: it is used as packing material; the straw can made into fuel, rope and toothpaste or formed into paper or bricks; the bran can be added to health foods, soap and cosmetics; the grain is used as animal feed, made into cereal, crackers, beer and more. What a plant!

When I was a kid, my dad couldn't stand casseroles of any form, or anything mixed together. So we had meat and a couple of miniscule vegetables. All I got in the realm of casseroles was the odd pasta dish. But my idea of a good time was chili, pot pies and those horrid '70s casseroles. What can I say? I'm the "saucy" type.

I like sauces on the side, on top, underneath and in a bowl for dipping. I also love all kinds of condiments, which you've no doubt noticed. If it's finger food and comes with a dip, I'm there. The great thing about these condiments is that most are just naturally vegetable-based. And the ones that normally aren't can easily be reworked into something more nutritious. And often more delicious.

I prefer homemade condiments to the fake taste of store-bought dressings. I think I first clued in on this when I tasted someone's homemade ketchup. It barely resembled the kind you buy. It was much less sweet, had way more herbs and spices, a deep rich flavor and a garden-fresh snap. Wow! Someday I swear I'll spend a whole day trying to replicate that recipe. I'm sure lots of cloves were involved.

I like to have a few homemade funky condiments on hand. If I didn't cook a lot, maybe I would be content with a few less. But I can use them up fairly quickly. Most are simple enough to whip up fresh whenever you need them anyway.

These recipes will help you out when you just need a little extra something to push your dish over the top.

FUNDERFUL CONDIMENTS

Miso Gravy

MAKES ABOUT 4 CUPS

This is becoming a cult thing. Every person or restaurant doing vegan seems to have his or her own version of this, many of them addictive. Use it alongside or over anything you darn well please, from fries to stuffing, from steamed veggies to rice.

5 cloves garlic, chopped
1 medium onion, chopped
1 Tbsp (15 mL) of olive oil
2 cups (500 mL) canned navy or other white beans
1 cup (250 mL) of unsweetened soy milk
2 Tbsp (30 mL) miso
salt and pepper to taste
1 tsp (5 mL) chopped fresh or dried green herb of your choice (parsley, oregano, basil, etc.)
salt and pepper to taste

Put about ¼ cup (60 mL) of water with the garlic, onion and olive oil into a saucepan. Cook on high, stirring constantly, until the onions are translucent. Add all the remaining ingredients (except for the salt and pepper) and simmer on low for 15 minutes. Remove from the heat and blend to smoothness with an upright or hand blender. Taste it before adding any salt; miso is salty and it may not need any. If you want it to be thicker, continue cooking on low.

Miso gravy is incredible with sesame fries or any kind of potatoes.

You can also refrigerate miso gravy and use it as a sandwich spread. It's a nice replacement for mayonnaise, even though the taste is completely different.

Because of its fermented flavor and incredible variations, miso is judged in Japan the way we judge fine wine and cheese.

Miso contains protein, calcium, iron and zinc. It's perfect for flavoring things like gravies and sauces. It doesn't always have to be the star—it makes a nice undertone for other flavors too.

Bonanza Barbecue Sauce

MAKES ABOUT 2 CUPS

This barbecue sauce is rich and thick. It's not the lowest fat recipe around, but it's decadent and most people love it. It's tangy, it's garlicky—it really is the best barbecue sauce. No need for fancy sweet stuff or exotic ingredients here. This packs huge flavor and you can whip it up lightning-quick!

1 cup (250 mL) ketchup
1 heaping Tbsp (15 mL) mustard
½ cup (125 mL) dark soy sauce
6 cloves garlic, finely chopped
2 Tbsp (30 mL) extra virgin olive oil

Simply combine the above ingredients. This makes a great quick and simple sauce for dipping fries or tofu fries, or spreading on whatever you like to grill.

You can also gently heat this up in a pan to serve with mini veggie burgers and dip them. You can also use this as the topping for a vegan meatloaf.

This barbecue sauce is the perfect marinade for anything you want to barbecue. You may have to thin it down to get it the consistency you want and for that you could use citrus juices, teriyaki sauce, more soy, wine, etc.

The ketchup lends this plenty of sweetness but this leans more in the garlic direction. But if you're a sweetie-type, add some dark blackstrap molasses, or some brown rice syrup or barley malt syrup. They give a sweet note and richness.

It's good to whip up a bottle of this for the week ahead, especially in the summer. Then it's ready for adding to burgers, as a marinade component, for dipping fries, zucchini sticks, tofu "fries" and other delicious things.

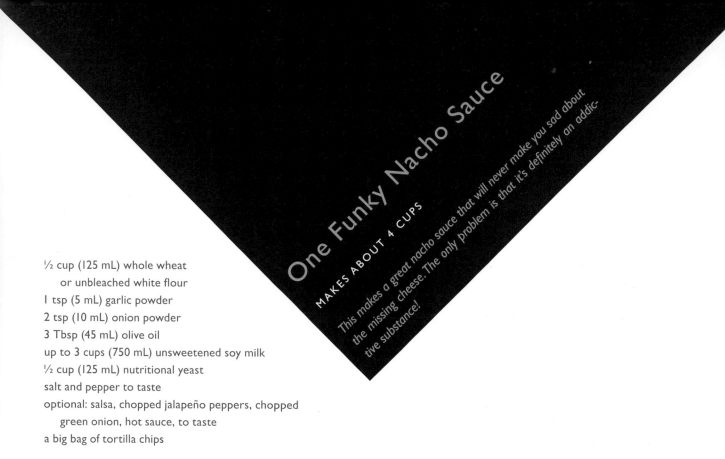

One Funky Nacho Sauce

MAKES ABOUT 4 CUPS

This makes a great nacho sauce that will never make you sad about the missing cheese. The only problem is that it's definitely an addictive substance!

½ cup (125 mL) whole wheat
   or unbleached white flour
1 tsp (5 mL) garlic powder
2 tsp (10 mL) onion powder
3 Tbsp (45 mL) olive oil
up to 3 cups (750 mL) unsweetened soy milk
½ cup (125 mL) nutritional yeast
salt and pepper to taste
optional: salsa, chopped jalapeño peppers, chopped
   green onion, hot sauce, to taste
a big bag of tortilla chips

Preheat oven to 350°F (180°C).

Combine the flour and garlic and onion powders well. In a saucepan, heat about 1 Tbsp (15 mL) olive oil on high. Add about ⅓ of the flour, whisking constantly. Add about ¼ cup (175 mL) soy milk at a time. Keep whisking. Add alternating oil, flour and water, continuing to whisk. Make sure the flour mixture comes to a boil for at least a minute or so with each flour addition. When it's the consistency of a cheese sauce turn the heat to low. Add the nutritional yeast. Taste it and season it with salt and pepper. Remove it from the heat.

If you want extra zing, add some salsa (and/or some chopped jalapeño peppers, some chopped green onion or hot sauce to your taste).

This is the ultimate poured over tortilla chips. Add whatever yummy tidbits (such as tomatoes, onions and olives) you like on nachos. You can eat them as is, or pop them into the oven on 350°F (180°C) until they're warm (5 minutes).

Strangely enough, you can also use filtered water, instead of the soy milk! I did that once when I was out of unsweetened soy milk. I thought it might be disgusting—not rich enough. The opposite was true; the flavor was sharper and it had a translucent quality that was somehow more cheese-like.

If you're the spicy type, add a few squirts of sriracha, or any hot sauce to make this nacho sauce deliciously hot. This makes a great dipping sauce for fries too. Another addiction!

Nutritional yeast is loaded with vitamins and there's some evidence that it's great for skin. A lot of people force themselves to drink it in a shake, but it's so yummy on savory things—why suffer? Just eat it.

Supreme Spinach Pesto

MAKES ABOUT 4 CUPS

There are lots of pestos out there and some include spinach. You can add as much spinach as you wish, but I like A LOT. It makes for a very flavorful and affordable pesto. This one calls for some basil, but if you can't get it fresh, just add a pinch of dried.

1 cup (250 mL) of your best extra
    virgin olive oil

⅓ cup (75 mL) lemon juice

1 clove garlic (for the tame!) or 6 cloves, chopped

2 green onions, chopped

½ cup (125 mL) pine nuts (traditional) or
    blanched almonds

salt and pepper to taste

½ cup (125 mL) fresh parsley, finely chopped

5 cups (1.25 L) fresh spinach leaves

½ cup (125 mL) basil leaves (or a pinch of dried basil)

The best way to do this is in a food processor: just dump all of the ingredients in, adding the leafy things last. Then pulse until it reaches the consistency you like. If you don't have a food processor, don't let that stop you! You could crush everything with a mortar and pestle, except the leaves. You could chop those as finely as possible with a sharp knife. If all else fails, just chop it all as finely as you can. People made these dishes long before we had all the gadgets!

This stuff is delicious. To buy any kind of store-bought pesto is pretty pricey, so it's completely worth your time to make it. You'll know that for sure when you taste it. The burst of fresh flavor will convince you!

When making your own pesto, experiment with different kinds of nuts. They all have their own personality and are all tasty additions. You only need a few to add richness.

Traditional basil pesto is the best, but try it with any greens you have. You can make a super fresh and fragrant one with just flat-leaf parsley as your green component.

Gorgeous Guacamole

MAKES ABOUT 2½ CUPS

If you like avocados, there's no more perfect a showcase for them than this amazing sauce, or dip. Try this on chips, toast or to use alongside anything with Southwestern flavors.

2 ripe avocados
¼ cup (60 mL) of fresh lime or lemon juice
salt and pepper to taste
1 clove garlic, finely chopped
1 green onion, finely chopped
1 tomato, finely chopped

Some people like this cool green dip to be ultra smooth, but I'll never understand the charm of that. Avocado has a great texture, and I'd hate to lose that by completely puréeing it.

Gently combine all of the ingredients, except the tomatoes, lightly mashing with a fork. Add the tomatoes and stir. Serve with warm tortilla chips, on a warm bean burrito or taco or on shredded lettuce. Fiesta time!

A lot of people have never had fresh, homemade guacamole. They've only had the store-bought kind with a lot of chemicals, or the kind with a lot of mayo added. They'll be pleasantly surprised at the intensity of this, made with ripe avocados.

Avocados have more Vitamin E than any other fruit. Many cultures believe that avocados have anti-aging properties.

Avocados also have the most phytochemicals of any fruit. They contain heart-healthy fats that lower LDL (bad) cholesterol. They have fiber, magnesium, folate and potassium, as well as beta-sitosterol, which lowers blood cholesterol.

To ripen an avocado, put it in a paper bag with a banana. Yes, it has to be a paper bag and it usually works overnight.

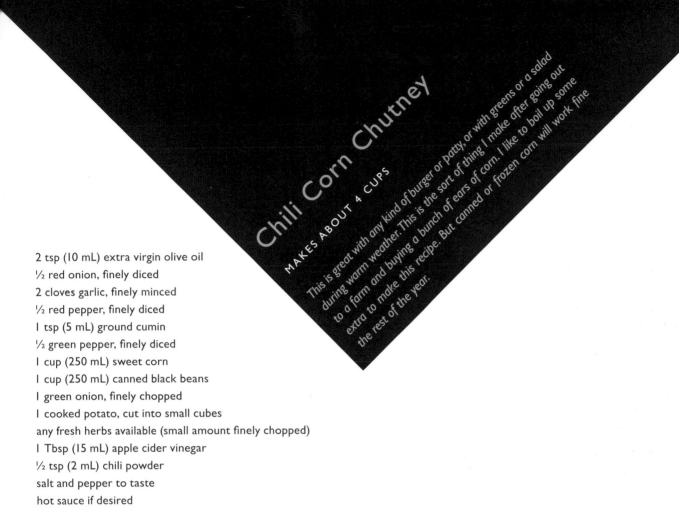

Chili Corn Chutney

MAKES ABOUT 4 CUPS

This is great with any kind of burger or patty, or with greens or a salad during warm weather. This is the sort of thing I make after going out to a farm and buying a bunch of ears of corn. I like to boil up some extra to make this recipe. But canned or frozen corn will work fine the rest of the year.

2 tsp (10 mL) extra virgin olive oil
½ red onion, finely diced
2 cloves garlic, finely minced
½ red pepper, finely diced
1 tsp (5 mL) ground cumin
½ green pepper, finely diced
1 cup (250 mL) sweet corn
1 cup (250 mL) canned black beans
1 green onion, finely chopped
1 cooked potato, cut into small cubes
any fresh herbs available (small amount finely chopped)
1 Tbsp (15 mL) apple cider vinegar
½ tsp (2 mL) chili powder
salt and pepper to taste
hot sauce if desired

Heat the olive oil in a pan over medium high heat. Add the onion, garlic and peppers and sauté. Set aside. In a bowl, combine the remaining ingredients, except the chili powder and salt and pepper. Add the sautéed mixture to the bowl and mix well. Sprinkle with the chili powder and give it one more quick mix. Season with salt and pepper and hot sauce, if desired. Chill for a delightfully cold side dish, or heat it up and serve it alongside whole grain dishes. This makes a complete meal in itself, served over a bed of chopped greens.

If you want to dive into the wonderful world of chutneys, check out Indian recipes. They have sweet ginger chutney, coconut, carrot pickle, apple pickle, peanut and mint chutneys—a wild bunch of condiments.

Typical chutney components include coconut, mangoes, apples, pears, tamarind, tomatoes, mint, ginger, garlic, honey, citrus fruits, cilantro and hot chillies. Make up your own new chutney—it might be the best one yet.

Roasted Tomato Chutney

Roasting anything is a terrific way to bring out flavor. Originally, I created this recipe for a condiment for veggie burgers, which is delicious. The sweet burst of the cherry tomatoes with the garlic and onions— mmmmm. If you're lucky enough to get ahold of the little yellow tomatoes, those are awesome roasted too.

2 cups (500 mL) cherry tomatoes

1 large onion, finely chopped

1 bulb garlic, finely chopped

½ mango, finely chopped

2 jalapeño peppers, finely chopped

1 cup (250 mL) flat-leaf parsley, finely chopped

generous drizzle of olive oil

salt and pepper to taste

1 tsp (5 mL) ground cumin

1 tsp (5 mL) curry powder

1 tsp (5 mL) tarragon

Optional: hot sauce, pinch of cinnamon, oregano

Preheat oven to 300°F (150°C).

Simply combine all of the ingredients and place them on a baking sheet lined with parchment. Bake for about 40 minutes, turning several times along the way. The chutney is done when the tomatoes are golden and the onions are translucent.

You can serve this with chips or crackers instead of the antipasto style dips. Or you can add some finely chopped jalapeños or other chili peppers to it and it'll be perfect with warmed corn tortilla chips. This chutney, along with some hummus and a few organic greens would make a fantastic sandwich.

Little tomatoes also come in that bright golden yellow—they're heavenly. If you know a gardener, maybe you could get some, perhaps by promising some luscious roasted tomato chutney in return for the incredible little candy-like tomatoes.

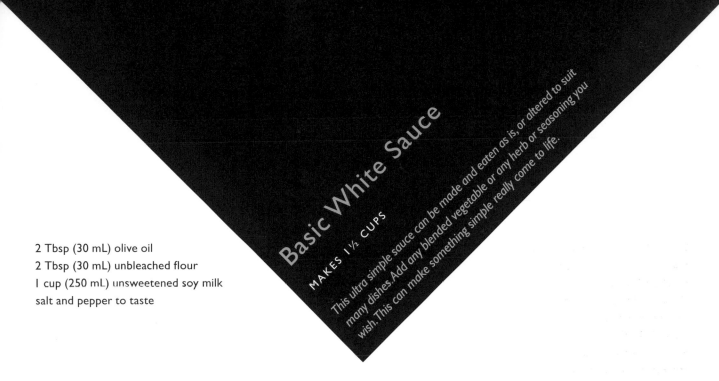

Basic White Sauce

MAKES 1 ½ CUPS

This ultra simple sauce can be made and eaten as is, or altered to suit many dishes. Add any blended vegetable or any herb or seasoning you wish. This can make something simple really come to life.

2 Tbsp (30 mL) olive oil
2 Tbsp (30 mL) unbleached flour
1 cup (250 mL) unsweetened soy milk
salt and pepper to taste

Heat the oil in a pan and immediately add the flour. Whisking constantly, cook for a couple of minutes on medium heat. Slowly add the soy milk a bit at a time, while whisking, so that the sauce is velvety smooth. Keep whisking and bring it up to a low boil, then turn it down immediately to low. Keep it on low heat if you want it to thicken further. Otherwise, season and cover it.

Add half of a finely chopped tomato and a pinch of saffron or finely grated lemon rind for a gorgeous aioli (flavored "mayonnaise"). Chill. Use as a condiment for burgers or anything you like.

Simmer on low to thicken the sauce. Then add ½ cup (125 mL) finely chopped, fresh dill. Serve it alongside salads, grain dishes, etc.

Replace the soy milk with your favorite white wine and add a lot of chopped, fresh green herbs—gorgeous!

Kidfood isn't that different from adult food—it should all look good and be fun. Kids are usually open-minded, and as long as you keep giving them options, they'll discover new things they love.

Be aware that it is adults, not children, who often put negative food connotations into kids' heads. From raising vegan kids I've heard adults say things like, "What's that you're eating? Kidney beans? Yuk. C'mon over to my house and I'll give you some ice cream."

There's a lot of twisted food psychology out there, including advertising to try to lure your kid into eating garbage. You CAN get them to love healthy foods. A huge part of nurturing this attitude toward food is the atmosphere you create.

Give kids great thoughts about food—that way they won't turn to the junk. For example, I'm not above calling all kinds of healthy foods "treats." Why should watermelon, for example, not be called a treat? It's often more expensive than candy, it's sweet and you can't get a good one year-round.

The wording is everything. *Super Bunny carrots* are much more fun, for example, than just *carrots*. Remind them of how much animals LOVE eating their vegetables—hamsters and mice would rather eat lettuce or greens more than anything and the silverback gorilla (one of nature's most powerful creatures) is a vegetarian.

Kids are also crazy about getting "the right" cup or bowl—they'll fight over the one in the color they like. Now there are so many reasonably priced kid implements that you should have no problem finding something they adore.

Although all of this takes time, your child's attitude toward food is being created today. So is his/her cell structure; it really is that important. There's really no better gift you can give a kid than turning him/her on to a path of enjoying the right foods.

KIDFOOD

Kid Pasta Supreme

Here's something for the kid in your life whether he or she is 6, 16 or 60. This is something I make for my kids to replace those junk-foody canned pastas I liked as a kid. (I can't believe I ever liked them—talk about the antithesis of al dente!) There's the odd edible one that doesn't contain cheese, but they're usually overpriced and not that great. This is a simple, tasty version.

2 cups cooked pasta (always
    cooked al dente)—pick a fun shape
    such as rotini, wagon wheels or bows
1 clove garlic, finely minced
1 small onion, finely chopped
1 Tbsp (15 mL) olive oil
1 cup (250 mL) of any vegetable that the child you're
    cooking for adores (corn, broccoli, beans, carrots,
    whatever), cooked or canned
½ cup (125 mL) vegetarian ground "beef" OR
    2 vegetarian hot dogs, cut into ½-inch (1 cm) "pennies"
oregano and basil, a good pinch of each
1 cup (250 mL) tomato sauce

Cook the garlic and onions in the olive oil on medium heat, stirring them well until the onions are translucent. Add a little water, if necessary, to get them tender. THEN, you're going to be a little tricky. Use a hand blender and whiz them up so that you can't see any chunks. Have you noticed that kids will accept onion chunks on a fast food hamburger, but at home the scrutiny is more intense? Anyway, if your kid likes onion bits, skip this step! The main point is to ensure that kids get food that's big on flavor. Put the onion/garlic mixture into a pot with all the other ingredients and cook until it's hot. You can serve this in a hollowed out bun and bake in a 200°F (95°C) oven for a few minutes until crispy. Or serve it in a red or green pepper that's had the top sliced off and rinsed out.

This is more work than buying the little cans of pasta in the store, but read the labels and I know you'll agree it's worth the effort. You can absolutely make a big batch of this and freeze it in small containers.

The word pasta comes from the Italian word for paste (flour and water—makes sense).

There are more than 600 different pasta shapes made worldwide, which certainly says something about its popularity.

You can get lovely whole grain pastas now. You can even get corn pasta. It cooks ultra fast and to have a completely delicious sauce that goes perfectly—just heat up some salsa.

Pasta 'n kids mix: since it comes in so many crazy shapes, kids tend to love eating pasta.

Baby Pasta Soup

SERVES 4–6 BABIES

This soup is perfect for babies and small children. The tiny pasta shapes are fun—you can use pastina (teeny balls), stellini (little stars), orzo, little bows, flowers, etc.

4 cups (1 L) vegetable stock
1½ cups (375 mL) little pasta shapes

Heat up the stock or boil 4 cups (1L) water and add the bouillon according to package instructions. Add the pasta and boil to desired consistency.

For babies, cool to lukewarm and if desired, drizzle with a dot of olive oil.

This recipe is simple, delicious and little kids love it.

There are several ways to make vegetable stock: You can make stock with a couple of good bouillon cubes. You'll have to read labels since many contain hydrogenated oils and other things that aren't fit for human consumption. You may have to get them in a health food store. Or find a decent ready-made stock, either canned or in cartons.

You can also add some small canned or cooked vegetables such as peas, corn, red pepper, carrots or beans to the broth to add extra color and interest.

Quickie Kid's Plate

SERVES 2

This is a once-in-a-while type of recipe; it's vegetarian fast food! You still want to give your kid something fun and not too horrific nutrition wise. As for the veg wieners, read the labels. They're all processed food, but some are better than others. Get the best out there.

4 veggie hot dogs

2–4 slices of good whole wheat bread

2 pickles, sliced into rings

mustard or honey† mustard

½ cup (125 mL) of a favorite kid vegetable

½ cup (125 mL) of another fave kid veggie

several cherry or grape tomatoes

6 carrot and/or celery sticks

2 Tbsp (30 mL) of any or all of the following: peanuts,
     other nuts, raisins, etc

several pretzels

Boil the hot dogs and the vegetables in one pot. Use common sense. Obviously this won't work if your kid's favorite vegetable is creamed corn!

Cut the hot dogs in ½-inch (1-cm) "pennies" and the bread in strips. Wrap the bread around the hot dog pieces and hold them together with toothpicks (if your child is old enough) or just pinch them closed. Dot or line them with mustard or ketchup.

Use your most awesomely colorful plate. Decorate it with the mini hot dogs, the carrots and celery sticks, and all the other little funky tidbits: sticks, tomatoes, nuts, raisins, etc.

† VEGAN OPTION agave syrup, brown rice syrup or barley malt syrup

Write a quick note to your special kid, roll it up and hide it in the napkin or poking out of one of the small dishes.

Some soy yogurt topped with berries, or a fresh fruit popsicle would make a good dessert.

I know people who aren't vegans or vegetarians, but buy the veggie hot dogs just because they're healthier. I find that the brand I use tastes exactly like the ones I remember eating as a kid; there's just a bit of a texture difference.

A Dutch fellow named William Beukelz who made pickled fish had his name mispronounced by English speakers and that's how the name "pickle" came about. This was waaay back in the 1300s.

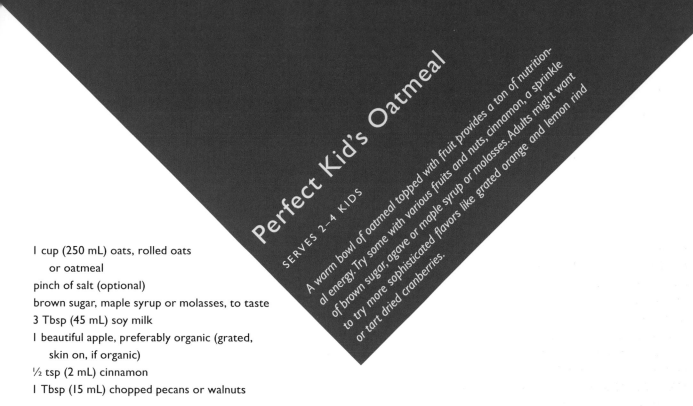

Perfect Kid's Oatmeal

SERVES 2–4 KIDS

A warm bowl of oatmeal topped with fruit provides a ton of nutritional energy. Try some with various fruits and nuts, cinnamon, a sprinkle of brown sugar, agave or maple syrup or molasses. Adults might want to try more sophisticated flavors like grated orange and lemon rind or tart dried cranberries.

1 cup (250 mL) oats, rolled oats
    or oatmeal
pinch of salt (optional)
brown sugar, maple syrup or molasses, to taste
3 Tbsp (45 mL) soy milk
1 beautiful apple, preferably organic (grated,
    skin on, if organic)
½ tsp (2 mL) cinnamon
1 Tbsp (15 mL) chopped pecans or walnuts

Boil 1½ cups of water, and add the oats. Add a pinch of salt if desired (it flavors it nicely). Turn it down to low and continue to cook, stirring every minute or so. Keep at a low simmer for about 5 minutes. If you wish to reduce the water more, simply cook it longer. If you want more liquid, add more water or soy milk. Or cover and let it sit (the oats will absorb more liquid while steaming in the pan).

Add a few spoonfuls of oatmeal to a bowl with lots of surface area. Add the brown sugar, maple syrup or molasses and stir it in well. Then add a bit of soy milk, stirring it in slightly. Grate the apple over the oatmeal (so the juice will sprinkle it). Add on nuts, cinnamon and a teeny bit more sugar on top. That's energy in a bowl.

Oatmeal is very filling and high in fiber, so it's good for dieters. Instead of some sugary cereal, go for a hot bowl of oatmeal with some fruit on top.

Other winning combinations are strawberries and almonds, strawberry-banana, banana-pecan, raisin and cinnamon, sunflower seeds with dried fruit bits, pineapple and coconut, blueberry-banana, etc.

The Peanut Butter Apple

SERVES 2

This fun, but messy, treat is a great alternative to a candy or a caramel apple. It's so stupidly simple you may wonder why I included it. First, it's full of great nutrition. Second, it's fabulous kid food that kids can create themselves. You can eat it as is, or elaborate to give it more eye appeal. Sometimes you just need one more little idea to get that after-school smile. Enjoy!

2 apples
2 Tbsp (30 mL) or more peanut butter
crushed almonds, toasted coconut, bits of
    dried fruit, sunflower seeds, etc. (optional)

Simply slather good peanut butter all over an apple. (Inserting a Popsicle stick or fork into the apple first will save you a sticky mess.) It can be eaten as is or rolled into coconut, nuts, etc.

OR

Cut the apple into slices. Put some peanut butter into a little dish for dipping. If you want to make it more like a dessert you could add a few drops of maple syrup or honey†, or a bit of soy yogurt and then whip. Serve the slices, dip and enjoy. This makes a perfect after-school snack, or lunch with a green salad on the side.

† **VEGAN OPTION** agave syrup, brown rice syrup or barley malt syrup

Try some of the other delicious nut butters if you haven't already. Cashew and almond butters are incredible. I've even seen a "Mystery Butter" with a combination of a lot of different nuts in the natural foods store. These don't contain any butter, by the way. The good ones contain just the nuts, ground up in their natural oils. Check the labels though, of course.

Whenever possible, get organic apples and don't peel them. Two-thirds of the fiber is in the peel. Also, it's loaded with antioxidants (so helps to reduce damage to cells).

The Peanut Butter Apple

Banana Delight

SERVES 2

This makes a terrific after-school snack. It's sweet, rich and dessert-like, yet packed with nutrition. Buy organic bananas. They're afford-able and the taste difference is phenomenal. I started buying them when my oldest daughter was a baby because she ate 4 bananas a day! They're firmer and actually have that intensely tropical banana smell. Yum!

2 ripe bananas
2 heaping Tbsp (30 mL) good
   peanut butter
2 Tbsp (30 mL) crushed almonds
   (or other nut)
2 Tbsp (30 mL) honey†

Cut up the banana into little circles, about 1 inch (2.5 cm) thick. Lay them out on a plate. Drizzle them with the honey (or vegan option), then spread the tops with peanut butter and dip them into the almonds. Serve immediately.

Adult Version: If you have no time to make a tempting dessert for a dinner party, do the same as above, with just enough peanut butter to make the almonds stick. Serve that swimming in a pool of Grand Marnier or Frangelico (the hazelnut flavor of this liqueur works perfectly with the peanut butter and almonds).

OR

Peel the bananas, cut them in half and soak them in the liqueur of your choice for about 15 minutes. Then coat them with crushed, toasted nuts of your choice and drizzle them with honey†. Why bake? You'll be amazed at how people freak out over this simple dessert.

† VEGAN OPTION agave syrup, brown rice syrup or barley malt syrup

Bananas are good for scholars: Eating bananas provides potassium, which makes the brain more alert, and more conducive to learning.

Instead of popping antacids for heartburn, try a banana. It has a naturally soothing effect. Bananas are also good for helping to regulate blood sugar levels, by giving the right boost and they contain Vitamin B6, which helps with that.

One Bowl Is Never Enough Popcorn

SERVES 4

This isn't only for the movies. It makes a nice snack any time. If you haven't tried popcorn without the butter, this might convince you that it can still be great. Try some as soon as possible.

Big bowl of air-popped popcorn
olive oil
1 cup (125 mL) nutritional yeast
good sea salt

If you've ever used an oil sprayer, you know the benefits. You get a nice, even coating and you use less oil. However, I got over my glee at using one pretty quickly. Since I make popcorn constantly, I got sick of inhaling great clouds of oil as I was spraying away. But if you can handle it, it's probably the best method for perfect popcorn.

You can also use the kind of bottle that drizzles nicely and just run it quickly over the whole surface of the popcorn, then sprinkle nutritional yeast and salt on it. Stir, then drizzle the oil again, then the nutritional yeast and salt. Repeat, tossing the popcorn around until it's all lightly flavored.

The olive oil makes the nutritional yeast and salt stick. And, of course, it mimics butter. Plain popped corn has a certain charm too though. For some (like me), nutritional yeast is an acquired taste. The first time my husband tried it, he was madly in love with it. I have non-vegetarian children come to my house who beg me for popcorn the minute they walk in the door, because they love this kind better than the traditional buttered variety.

Nutritional yeast is yellow, and comes in various forms from powdery to flaky. It has a fermented flavor somewhat comparable to cheese. It makes great cheese-like sauces and it's a fun flavoring to add to lots of things. I have one daughter who would eat it on everything if I let her!

Popcorn has to be one of the best diet foods of all time. If you have air-popped popcorn with no butters or oils, go for it anytime. Even with a light coating of oil and seasoning, it's still a better option than a lot of snack foods.

Popcorn with curry spices on it is to die for! It's actually hard to go back after having the spicy version.

If you're vegan or health-conscious, you know there's nothing for you to munch on at the movie theater. I just pack my own stuff and throw it in a bag—nobody has ever bugged me about it yet. If they had healthy popcorn there, I'd be happy to buy it.

I'm never going to be a breakfast person. Gimme coffee only, 'till noon. I do love breakfasty foods though. And I recognize the importance of eating breakfast so I always make something for my kids who are breakfast types. If you're semi-reasonable and don't eat past 8:00 p.m. in the evening (a good plan), you should be hungry in the morning.

So here are some suggestions to give you a little boost in the morning. Some are super-quick to get you out the door in a flash and all provide some decent nutrition for that much needed energy.

If you simply have no time for breakfast, pack a few raw nuts and dried fruits to munch on. Keep some trail mix or a decent granola bar in your car. Or toast some multi-grain bread the night before, drizzle it with a dot of olive oil, or pack a little hummus to spread on it—yum. Or just pack a banana. Just so you have SOMETHING if you need it. It might keep you from eating some junky fast food (not to mention spending the money).

Of course, these can be eaten any time of day. So I hope that you try these ideas or they spark some of your own. Happy sunrises!

BREAKFAST BITES

Tofu "Eggs"

SERVES 4

Every vegetarian seems to have a version of this recipe. Like miso gravy, it's just one of those great vegan basics. With this, you can create a quick Sunday brunch or a light evening meal any time.

2–3 Tbsp (30–45 mL) olive oil
1 medium onion, chopped or sliced
12-oz (350-g) block of firm tofu
¼ cup (60 mL) nutritional yeast
½ tsp (2 mL) garlic powder
1 tsp (5 mL) onion powder
salt and pepper to taste
drizzle of soy or teriyaki sauce
¼ cup (60 mL) fresh parsley, chopped

Put 1 Tbsp (15 mL) of oil and the onions in a pan on medium heat, stirring constantly, until the onions are translucent. Add the tofu and cut it into little bricks or cubes (it will scramble more as you cook) and continue to heat up. Add all of the ingredients and seasonings and any additional oil you wish. Flip it and cook it until all flavors are well incorporated. This should take a total of about 7–10 minutes, so it's a nice, quick meal. Turn it out on a platter and serve it with multi-grain toast or a hot plate of fast cooked greens.

I love to serve this with gai-lan (Chinese green vegetable). The soft tofu and the bright fresh greens are amazing together.

This tofu is great served on top of extra crispy toast that's lightly drizzled with olive oil.

French Toast Frenzy

SERVES 4–6

I love the idea of those leisurely Sunday brunches (the only day that I don't have to shoot out the door at the crack of dawn). The trouble is, I always have to squeeze a lot of other things in on Sunday and I don't get tons of time to do the big brunch thing. Here are two quick and easy versions.

2 cups (500 mL) soy milk
¼ cup (60 mL) orange juice
1 orange rind, grated
1 Tbsp (15 mL) pure maple syrup
1 tsp (5 mL) cinnamon
1 loaf of great multi-grain or whole wheat bread
olive oil for the pan, as needed
orange slices to decorate plates

Combine the soy milk, orange juice, orange rind, maple syrup and cinnamon. Using a brush or a spoon, coat a slice of bread with this mixture. Try to get a little of the flavor all over it, but don't saturate the bread until it's a soggy mess. Add a little bit of olive oil to a pan and heat. Grill each piece for about 20 seconds or until golden brown. Add a dot more oil to the pan and flip it. Grill until golden. Remove and lightly dust with powdered sugar. Decorate with orange slices or serve with other fruits if desired.

OR

The no-oil method also works well. Toast the bread first. Dip each side once quickly into the "milk" mixture. Again, don't saturate the bread. Place it on a baking sheet covered with parchment and cook it in a preheated 400°F (200°C) oven until firm, golden, and not wet in the middle. Flip each piece once. If you aren't worried about the calories, you can drizzle each slice with a bit of olive oil before cooking, for richness. Dust the toast with powdered sugar and decorate it with the orange slices.

Before you dust this with the sugar, you should taste it. You might love it as is, with its light sweetness and infusion of orange.

Medieval European cooks made French toast to liven up stale bread. Adding eggs and milk to it reconstituted the bread, then they cooked it in fat on a hot griddle.

You can flavor this French toast any way you like. I think cinnamon and orange gets you revved up in the morning, but think about all the possibilities.

V CUISINE

Superhero Morning Smoothie

SERVES 2

I've never been a breakfast fan (unless it's at noon). But my kids are starving the second they wake up, so I've gotten into that early food mode. This works well when you're on the run.

1 banana
1 orange
½ cup (60 mL) raspberries
   or strawberries
½ cup (60 mL) soy milk
1 tsp (5 mL) vanilla
½ tsp (2 mL) cinnamon
½ cup (125 mL) soy yogurt
1 Tbsp (15 mL) wheat germ
1 Tbsp (15 mL) malt powder (the stuff that made
   the special taste in old fashioned milkshakes) (optional)

Blend the above ingredients with an upright or hand blender. If you have time, chill it for five or ten more minutes before guzzling.

A great thing to do is to put this in one of the large stainless steel coffee cups with a lid and then take it with you when you jet out the door. You could have all the ingredients except the banana blended the night before and kept refrigerated in the blender bowl. Then just add the banana, whiz it up and go!

Throwing in some wheat germ is a good way to add protein and good carbs to a smoothie.

Brekkie Burrito

SERVES 2

This is a deliciously savory, high-energy breakfast for the spicy set. Might as well start your morning off on an exciting note.

2 Tbsp (30 mL) olive oil

1 green onion, finely chopped

½ tsp (2 mL) anise seeds

½ cup (125 mL) red pepper, finely chopped

2 crimini mushrooms, finely sliced

1 clove garlic, finely minced

½ cup (125 mL) firm or extra firm tofu, cut into cubes

½ cup (125 mL) cooked brown rice (or other whole grain)

2 tsp (10 mL) flaxseeds

salt and pepper to taste

hot sauce to taste

2 good flour or corn tortillas

Heat the olive oil in a pan and add the green onions, anise seeds, red pepper, mushrooms and garlic. Turn to high heat, stirring constantly. Cook until the white parts of the onion are translucent and the red pepper is cooked down. Add the tofu. Scramble it around in the pan with the veggies so the flavors meld. Add the brown rice and the flaxseeds.

Cook another minute or two, scrambling. Taste it and add the seasonings. Remove it from the heat. When it's cool enough, fill the tortillas with the mixture, making a line down the middle, ending about 2 inches (5 cm) from the edge. Fold the tortilla over, then tuck both ends in well and roll it up the rest of the way. If you want it really warm, wrap it in foil and bake at 350°F (180°C) for 5 minutes, to heat it up.

This is a winner! And who says you have to have it for breakfast? Eat it any time of day you like.

Burrito actually means "little burro" or "donkey." And a fried burrito is called a chimichanga.

You could replace the tofu here with black beans and it will be fantastic.

Hash Brown Heaven

SERVES 4–6

The key here is to start with some super delicious potatoes. I like Yukon Gold. You can also go for some perfect red skinned ones. Organic is best and they're wonderful with the skins on. If you boil the potatoes first, you won't have to check to see if the potatoes are cooked through. It's better in the long run.

5–6 potatoes, boiled to
    fork-tenderness
2 Tbsp (30 mL) olive oil
1 large onion, chopped super finely
1 green onion, finely chopped
1 Tbsp (15 mL) dried tarragon
salt and pepper to taste
parsley to garnish

Preheat oven to 450°F (230° C) or turn on broiler.

Cut the potatoes into smallish cubes. Add them to a bowl and drizzle them with the olive oil. Add the onion, green onion and the tarragon. Taste and season. At this point you could certainly add some hot sauce, lemon juice or any additional seasonings you like. If you have time to keep an eye on it, put them under the broiler on high. When they get golden brown on top, flip it all over and do the same on the other side. If you want super crunch, mix it well and do it one more time.

You can also just bake this at about 450°F (230°C) for about 20 minutes, flipping once when they're golden. Serve these alongside Tofu "Eggs," with a side of fresh salsa—killer! Garnish with parsley. A New Age cowboy-type breakfast.

Add lots of garlic, onion and hot sauce to a can of baked beans and bake. This goes perfectly with hash browns.

These are delicious with a bit of cumin tossed in before baking—the aroma is wild too.

These are also delicious added to a green salad—the heck with croutons.

Unreal Meatless Sausage Patties

SERVES 4–6

These are really delicious; they have the flavor of an Italian sausage without the grossness (I never used to like to think what was in that stuff—yuk. When I was a kid, we used to say "chicken lips"). There's olive oil present here, but you'll see that they're not even close to the greasiness of real sausages.

2 cups (500 mL) cooked brown rice
1 cup (250 mL) cooked, diced onion
6 cloves garlic, finely chopped
2 Tbsp (30 mL) olive oil
1 Tbsp (15 mL) anise seed
1 Tbsp (15 mL) Italian seasoning or
   oregano/basil combination
generous sprinkling of salt
1 tsp (5 mL) black pepper
1 Tbsp (15 mL) soy sauce
2 Tbsp (30 mL) fresh chopped parsley
1 green onion, finely diced
red pepper flakes, optional

Preheat oven to 425°F (220°C).

Combine the above ingredients in a mixing bowl. With a hand blender, break up the rice grains, until it resembles a hamburger-like consistency. With olive oiled hands, form into patties, balls or sausage shapes. Bake on a lightly olive oiled or parchment covered baking sheet until they're golden brown or firm to the touch.

You can serve these with barbecue sauce, or with a plate of steamed greens and some Chili Corn Chutney (page 169).

These also make great breakfast sausages with Tofu Eggs. That's a heavy-duty breakfast when you're going out to do something really energetic. It's a great meal for kids any time.

If you prefer a milder "sausage," just go easy on the pepper. And perhaps introduce the anise seed slowly, starting with just 1 tsp (2 mL), as it's an unusual flavoring for those not used to it.

Make these into little meatball shapes and simmer in some tomato sauce. Serve on lengthwise-sliced long buns or baguettes for a killer "meatball" sub!

When it comes to baking, the fresh stuff rules. Although I'm not a sweets freak, having kids and entertaining means I'm always on the lookout for a new cookie or cupcake recipe. I like things that are fast, simple and of course, taste great. Even the freshest bakery muffin isn't as great as one out of your oven.

I like making bread because the store-bought ones that contain decent ingredients are ridiculously expensive. I also like to make rustic looking breads, because if it doesn't *look* homemade, what's the point?

The recipes here are fairly simple and you can get a lot of mileage out of them. You can rework these recipes by adding different ingredients to achieve various flavors. The bread dough I use for almost everything is uncomplicated and you can turn it into a pizza crust, a tart base, pretzels, cinnamon buns—you name it.

Another happy side benefits to baking? Your place will smell divine! Who needs air fresheners or scented candles when the aroma of lemon rind and cinnamon stick is flowing from your oven?

BODACIOUS BAKING

Pretzels with Pizzazz

Making your own pretzels isn't as complicated as most people think. And there's really no substitute for fresh pretzels, hot out of the oven. I like them slathered with gobs of mustard. The dough from this recipe has multiple uses.

1 cup (250 mL) warm water

1 heaping tsp (5 mL) yeast

1 tsp (5 mL) sugar or honey†

3 cups (750 mL) flour (whole wheat or unbleached white)

coarse salt

any other toppings you might like to add such as sesame seeds, poppy seeds, sunflower seeds, bits of garlic or onion, pepper or even cinnamon and sugar

Preheat oven to 425°F (220°C).

The *only* trick to making dough is ensuring you have the right water temperature. It must be somewhere between lukewarm and warm, not cold or hot, which will kill the yeast.

Combine the water, yeast and honey or sugar. When the yeast is foamy, give it a stir and add in the first cups of flour. Continue adding flour as long as it's easy to stir in. Then begin to knead it in. Pour on some flour and push it in with the heel of your hand, give it a turn and repeat. When the bulk of the dough is no longer sticky, knead the dough for a few minutes. Then cover and put in a warm, dark place.

When the dough rises (say, 20 minutes or so) give it one more quick kneading (you'll probably have to add more flour, and flour your hands well). Divide the dough into 4 pieces. Then out of the first quarter of the dough, make 4–6 smaller dough balls. Take one piece at a time and make it into a long "rope," about 18 inches (46 cm) or so and form that into a pretzel shape or some other funky shape. Place your pretzel on a lightly oiled baking sheet.

Brush a little olive oil or water over the top of each pretzel and sprinkle it with salt (or whatever you desire). For a browner top, brush them with 1 tsp (5 mL) of baking soda dissolved in ¼ cup (60 mL) of water.

Pop these into the oven and remove them when they're golden brown.

† VEGAN OPTION agave syrup, brown rice syrup or barley malt syrup

Instead of yet another Valentine's Day cookie or cupcake, make heart shaped pretzels. Or spell out a special child's name, or your fiancé's. It's a nice change from the chocolate. There are people who will want to murder me for saying that.

Instead of mustard (although that's the ultimate combination) you can serve these with olive oil and balsamic vinegar, mixed on a flat plate for dipping. Or how about some Supreme Spinach Pesto (page 167)? Or any dip you love would be great.

Did you know German kids wear pretzels around their necks for good luck on New Year's!

Easy Blueberry Muffins

MAKES 12 GIANT MUFFINS

These muffins are dense and filling. If you make the big ones, be sure to use the largest cupcake paper liners. These make a great breakfast for kids—or for anyone, for that matter—with a glass of soy milk.

4 Tbsp (30 mL) olive oil
2 cups (500 mL) soy milk
½ cup (125 mL) maple syrup
2 tsp (4 mL) pure vanilla extract
3 cups (750 mL) whole wheat flour
1 cup (250 mL) cornmeal
2 Tbsp (30 mL) baking powder
½ tsp (2 mL) salt
½ tsp (2 mL) cinnamon
1½ cups (375 mL) blueberries, raspberries, blackberries or
    chopped strawberries (frozen is fine)

Preheat oven to 350°F (180°C).

Mix the above ingredients together. I've made them mixing the wet ingredients first, or the dry—just make sure it's all well incorporated and add the berries last.

Spoon batter into a muffin tin lined with paper liners and bake for 20–25 minutes (or a couple of minutes extra for the large). They're done when a knife or skewer poked into one comes out clean.

How about Rum-Raisin Muffins? Replace the vanilla with dark rum or rum extract and the berries with raisins.

Make 'em savory! Use unsweetened soy milk and replace the maple syrup with soy milk as well. Omit the cinnamon and blueberries and instead add: 1 tsp (5 mL) onion powder, ½ tsp (2 mL) rosemary and ½ cup (125 mL) finely chopped, fresh parsley. Mmmmm!

Muffins are a perfect place to pop in some cooked whole grains. Or just throw in some oats. Healthy muffins are a great way to start a day.

Tofu Carob Brownies

MAKES 9 LARGE BROWNIES

You might be surprised that these contain tofu, which keeps them moist. The flavor is rich and like a "normal" brownie. You could use vegan cocoa powder instead of the carob if you wish.

12-oz (350-g) package medium tofu

1 cup (250 mL) sugar

1 tsp (5 mL) pure vanilla extract

1 tsp (5 mL) cinnamon

¾ cup (175 mL) olive oil

1 cup (250 mL) chopped walnuts

¾ cup (175 mL) carob powder (or cocoa)

1 cup (250 mL) whole wheat flour

2 tsp (10 mL) baking soda

½ cup (125 mL) icing sugar

1 container vanilla non-dairy ice cream

2 Tbsp (30 mL) soy milk

Preheat oven to 350°F (180°C).

Put the tofu, sugar, vanilla, cinnamon and oil into a large bowl and whisk well. Add the walnuts, ½ cup (125 mL) of the carob powder, whole wheat flour and baking soda and mix well. The mixture should be the consistency of cake batter. If it's too thick, simply thin it a bit with water or soy milk. If it's too thin, then add a bit more flour.

Pour the mixture into a lightly oiled and flour dusted square or round 9-inch baking pan (1.5 L) (or one covered with parchment). Bake for 30 minutes or until the top is firm and a knife inserted in the middle comes out clean. Cool.

Take the remaining ¼ cup (60 mL) of carob powder and combine it with ½ cup (125 mL) of icing sugar. Add 2 Tbsp (30 mL) soy milk a bit at a time and mix it until it reaches a creamy icing consistency. Add a bit more soy milk if needed. Ice the brownies, cut them into squares and top them with nuts if desired.

Because of its moistness, tofu is another product that can replace oil or butter in baking.

Instead of the carob and soy milk in the icing, just use icing sugar, then slowly add a bit of strong coffee, mixing until you get a perfect icing consistency. If you're a mocha fan, you'll love it.

Put dark rum into a bowl, with a cinnamon stick. Dip each brownie in till the bottom is saturated. Plate it and scoop on some non-dairy ice cream. Then drizzle the top with a coffee or nut liqueur. An ultra-rich dessert for the grown ups.

Tofu Carob Brownies

Chewy Chompers

These are devilishly deadly. Nobody will know this is a vegan cookie— they're chewy, they're great, they're a little evil.

¾ cup (175 mL) olive oil

½ cup (125 mL) soy milk

2 Tbsp (30 mL) flaxseeds

2 cups (500 mL) dark brown sugar (loose, not packed)

¾ cup (175 mL) carob powder

1 tsp (5 mL) baking soda

1¼ cup (310 mL) slivered almonds or chopped macadamia nuts

¼ cup (60 mL) oat bran

1½ cups (375 mL) whole wheat flour

½ tsp (2 mL) coarse salt

Preheat oven to 350°F (180°C).

Combine the olive oil, flaxseeds and soy milk and whiz with a hand blender until smooth. Then mix in the sugar. Add the carob powder, stirring it well and pressing it against the sides of the bowl with a spoon to break up any chunks of carob powder. Add the baking soda, almonds and oat bran and combine well. Stir in the flour, ½ cup (125 mL) at a time. Add the salt and mix well. Make sure it's all incorporated. I'm not one to be a stickler for the necessity of salt in all baking, but it really enhances these.

Spoon the cookies onto a lightly greased baking sheet covered in parchment. Space the cookies 1 inch (2.5 cm) apart. A nice size is 1½–2 inches (4–5 cm) across, but make them the size you like. Bake for 20–25 minutes. Watch carefully to make sure they don't burn, but remember that carob does get quite dark when cooked. When you take them out, they still won't be super firm and may appear underdone. Remove the cookies from the oven and cool. They should firm up fast, and then enjoy!

If you aren't the nutty type, you could switch the almonds to dried cranberries, or dried sour cherries, if you're a Black Forest kind of a person.

For the holidays you can drizzle these with a stripe of white icing for contrast, with some crushed candy cane sprinkled into it.

You can also press this dough into a greased pie crust and bake it that way. It makes a magnificent ice cream cake. Just cover it with vegan vanilla ice cream and freeze it, or use frozen bananas whizzed up with soy milk and a pinch of cinnamon.

Gingerellas

As naughty as the sugar and oil may be, the flaxseeds, nuts and ginger are terrific for you. The bite of the ginger makes these cookies rock n' roll and the flaxseeds are ultra-healthy and give a richer flavor. Sweet!

9 Tbsp (135 mL) flaxseeds
½ cup (125 mL) soy milk
¾ (175 mL) cup olive oil
2 cups (500 mL) dark brown sugar
1 tsp (5 mL) pure vanilla extract
1 cup (250 mL) crushed almonds
2 Tbsp (30 mL) wheat germ or oat bran
½ cup (125 mL) crushed pecans or walnuts
½ tsp (2 mL) salt
1 tsp (5 mL) baking soda
3 Tbsp (45 mL) powdered ginger
1¼ cup (310 mL) whole wheat flour

Preheat oven to 350°F (180°C).

Blend the flaxseeds and the soy milk together in a bowl with an upright or hand blender until you get a greyish flax "butter." Add the olive oil, brown sugar and vanilla and mix well.

Add the remaining ingredients, except for the flour, and combine. Then add the flour. I like to add the flour in slowly—it's easier. Prepare a cookie sheet (lightly oiled or lined with parchment). Spoon onto the cookie sheet, leaving 1 inch (2.5 cm) or so between cookies. If you want, you can flatten them a little. Bake in a preheated 350°F (180°C) oven for about 20 minutes. Let cool for a few minutes—they'll harden up.

These are spicy and yummy. For a real walk on the wild side, serve with Cocoa Mexicana (page 201)!

Make some ginger tea. Just a chunk of ginger boiled in water can give you a lift in the morning. It's great for digestion too.

This flaxseed "butter" can be used in a million ways. Add a pinch of salt to it and spread it on your morning toast. Use it in dips and spreads, and certainly in baked goods.

If you want to put these over the top, you could press some chunks of candied ginger into the top of these before baking.

I'm not a sweets chick. Gimme something garlicky or salty any day! I'm enthusiastic about making great sweets, though. And while I may not have the most discerning taste buds in this area, I have people to test the stuff on.

I realize that some people think that sweet stuff should be naughty—it's part of the appeal. And I'm not telling you there's no sinful element to these. Some seem a little evil, but compared to the usual dessert fare, this stuff is lean and mean! So if you choose to partake, you won't have to agonize.

Creating beautiful desserts is limited only by the imagination. Sugar can be sculpted in almost any way you like. You can indulge all of your desires for fruity flavors or other tastes that mingle with the sweet. My favorite desserts are cold—a non-dairy ice cream loaded with a crazy amount of vanilla bean, or frozen banana slices that have been dipped in carob and encrusted with nuts.

Here is a simple parfait that looks gorgeous. I've also included no-bake desserts, which are not only in a more natural state than baked goods, they're easy to make. I've tried to give you a multitude of textures so you have options according to your mood. Plus, a few of the foodie trends are indulged here. Sweets encompass so many flavors—you can really let your imagination fly.

You can start with a simple piece of cake and dress it up in a million different ways. Or you can begin with gorgeous fruit in season and build from there. Just putting that fruit in a fancy glass and eating it with a spoon makes it dessert.

Sweets are about attitude. You get to invoke a feeling of indulgence, richness and yes, that sweet naughtiness. It's fun in a devilish way.

Whether you go for a simple fruit concoction, a rich pie or a tangy tart, I hope you find these desserts fun, easy to prepare and decadent enough to dazzle.

Strawberries with Balsamic

SERVES 4

I have no idea who started this strawberry balsamic thing (probably someone in Italy who we'll never know about). It's such a perfect and brilliant combination that I had to include it. You can add more sweetness if you wish, but if you have ripe strawberries, you won't need to. The balsamic vinegar, although tangy, has an intense sweetness, and the combination is beyond description. Please try it—when strawberries are in season, of course. And bravo to the experimental soul who started it all!

2 cups (500 mL) ripe, rich, red
    strawberries
2 Tbsp (30 mL) balsamic vinegar
1 tsp (5 mL) sugar or honey†

Cut the strawberries into fine slices. Pour over the balsamic vinegar and the honey or sugar. Mix well. Let it sit for half an hour before serving. Magnificent!

† VEGAN OPTION agave syrup, brown rice syrup or barley malt syrup

Instead of adding the sweetness, just dust the top of your strawberries and balsamic with a hint of icing sugar, the lightest dusting possible. You can use a fine strainer to make a fine coating of the icing sugar, just a hint, like the lightest of snow flurries.

Since balsamic is the quintessential Italian ingredient, you could make this more decadent with pine nuts, if desired.

Traditional balsamic vinegar must be at least 12 years old. Some of the balsamic vinegar sold on supermarket shelves is wine vinegar with a bit of true balsamic added to flavor it.

Put pure balsamic vinegar into a saucepan and heat it on low until it's greatly reduced, thick and syrupy. This balsamic reduction is a fantastic drizzle for sweet and savory dishes alike.

Cocoa Mexicana

SERVES 4

I'm not sure what it is about this stuff, but people tend to go wild over it. It's sweet, it's spicy and super-rich. It's that little pinch of cayenne pepper that gives it the fierce flavor, that Mexican flair.

½ cup (125 mL) carob powder
¼ cup (60 mL) dark brown sugar
4 cups (1 L) soy milk
pinch of cayenne pepper, or to taste
2 cinnamon sticks
pinch of ground cloves or freshly grated nutmeg
    (optional)
non-dairy vanilla ice cream (optional)

Combine the carob powder and the sugar, then slowly add the soy milk, until it reaches a smooth consistency. You may need to blend it up with a hand or upright blender. Stir in the cayenne, cinnamon sticks and cloves/nutmeg if desired. Heat the cocoa in a saucepan over medium-low heat until it comes to a boil, stirring as it heats up. Serve it immediately, with a scoop of the ice cream on top, if you wish.

Traditionally this is made in a double boiler. I haven't found a need for that—as long as you bring it up to a boil slowly, continuously stirring when it begins to get hot.

The Aztecs and Mayans made a chocolate drink they considered sacred. They used it in their ceremonies. It was ultra-dark, rich, spicy and made with water as the base. It was unsweetened and often had crushed hot peppers in it, along with other spices.

To make regular cocoa (not spicy) for you, or for kids, do the same recipe as above, minus the cayenne, and leave the nutmeg and cloves optional (some people would prefer it simpler). You might also want to go lighter on the carob, depending on the person. Just use ¼ cup and add extra if desired.

You can make "vanilla cocoa" by adding a dash of vanilla and omitting the carob powder completely. Serve it with a scoop of carob non-dairy ice cream (yes, there is such a thing available in specialty natural food stores).

When you're not doing the hot spice, try a drop or two of pure peppermint extract with your cocoa. It'll taste like a Peppermint Patty.

V CUISINE

Maple Pumpkin-Stuffed Vanilla Pears

SERVES 8

Since I have a thing for vanilla beans, I'm always looking for a place to add some in recipes. Also, I like to have a few special holiday recipes and this is one of those. I love the look of poached fruits and the way you can infuse flavors into them, with additions to the poaching water. Plus, I like things with a filling! So this is the kind of holiday recipe I can get into. It's easy too.

4 organic pears, halved (skin on)
½ cup (250 mL) + 1 Tbsp (15 mL)
    dark rum
1 vanilla bean
1 cup (250 mL) brown sugar
2 cups (500 mL) pumpkin purée
1 tsp (5 mL) pure maple syrup
pinch of cinnamon
pinch of ground cloves
1 cup (250 mL) dried cranberries
1 cup (250 mL) toasted slivered almonds

Put the pears in a pot with ½ cup (250 mL) of dark rum and add enough water to cover. Add the vanilla bean (seeds removed and reserved) and the brown sugar. Bring it to a boil and then turn the heat down to simmer.

Simmer for about 15–20 minutes, until the pears are fork tender. You may want to check along the way since different varieties and sizes of pears cook differently.

Stir together the pumpkin purée, maple syrup, cinnamon, cloves and all the seeds of the vanilla bean. Remove the pears from the heat. If there isn't enough of a well to put in the filling, lightly scoop pear halves with a small spoon. Fill them with the pumpkin mixture. Sprinkle them with cranberries and toasted almonds. Serve with non-dairy vanilla ice cream, if desired.

If you can get some gorgeous red skinned pears, they look incredible and are delicious.

I love these served in summer but instead of bothering with the pumpkin purée, I just fill them with vegan vanilla ice cream and pour fresh raspberries or blackberries over the top. Gorgeous.

A vanilla bean is the seed pod from a vanilla orchid. The world's largest producer of vanilla beans is Madagascar.

Maple syrup can be used to flavor all kinds of things instead of sugar. With its intensely tasty sweetness, you only require a small amount to get a decadent result.

Amazing Tofu Cheesecake

There are people who will think I'm 100% insane for saying this, but I actually like this better than "real" cheesecake. There's enough flavor going on here with the tang of the pineapple for the tofu to work perfectly.

CRUST

2 cups (500 mL) crushed cashews, or any nuts you like
1 Tbsp (15 mL) carob powder
1 cup (250 mL) wheat germ or bran
2 Tbsp (30 mL) peanut butter
2 Tbsp (30 mL) honey† or molasses

FILLING

12 oz (350 g) block firm tofu
10 oz (284 mL) can pineapple, juice drained
1 tsp (5 mL) vanilla or lemon extract
¼ cup (60 mL) maple syrup
½ tsp (2 mL) cinnamon

TOPPING

2 cups of canned, fresh or frozen (thawed) fruit or berries, whatever you like

For the crust: combine all of the above ingredients together (mix by hand or use a food processor) and then simply press it down into a lightly olive oiled 9-inch (1.5-L) pie plate. Cover with plastic wrap and chill for an hour.

For the filling: remove the plastic from the chilled crust. Spread the filling into it. Cover it again and chill it for at least another hour.

Spoon on the topping just before serving—you can add a sprinkle of powdered sugar, another drizzle of maple syrup or a dusting of carob powder as desired.

† **VEGAN OPTION** agave syrup, brown rice syrup or barley malt syrup

Tofu is low in calories and saturated fat and has no cholesterol. It's power-packed with B vitamins, iron, calcium, protein and amino acids.

Cheesecakes these days come in so many gourmet flavors, from Tiramisu to Chai Latte. That's why tofu works so well as a cheesecake base—it picks up flavors perfectly.

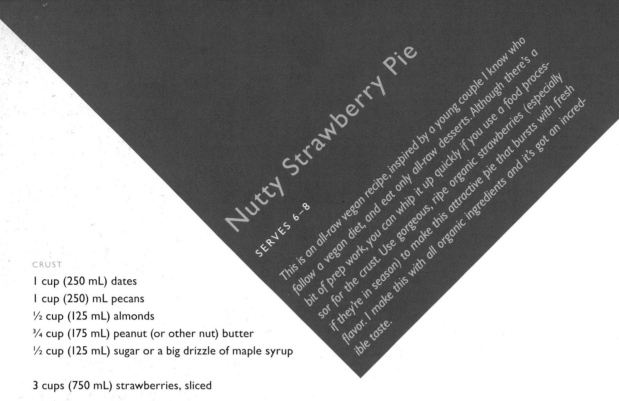

Nutty Strawberry Pie

SERVES 6–8

This is an all-raw vegan recipe, inspired by a young couple I know who follow a vegan diet, and eat only all-raw desserts. Although there's a bit of prep work, you can whip it up quickly if you use a food processor for the crust. Use gorgeous, ripe organic strawberries (especially if they're in season) to make this attractive pie that bursts with fresh flavor. I make this with all organic ingredients and it's got an incredible taste.

CRUST

1 cup (250 mL) dates
1 cup (250) mL pecans
½ cup (125 mL) almonds
¾ cup (175 mL) peanut (or other nut) butter
½ cup (125 mL) sugar or a big drizzle of maple syrup

3 cups (750 mL) strawberries, sliced

FILLING

1½ cups (375 mL) shaved almonds
½ cup (125 mL) sugar
soy milk to cover, about ¾ cup (175 mL)
½ cup (125 mL) soy yogurt (vanilla or strawberry)
several strawberries cut in half to decorate the top

For the crust: chop the crust ingredients as finely as you can, or put them into a food processor and pulse them until they all stick together. Lightly olive oil a 9-inch (1.5-L) pie plate and then press the mixture into the pan, from the middle out, and up the sides.

Layer the sliced strawberries at the bottom of the pie crust.

For the filling: combine the shaved almonds, the sugar and the soy milk. With an upright or hand blender, whiz it to the consistency of a thick pudding. Mix in the yogurt and spread it over the strawberries to cover and fill the pie crust. Decorate the top with the remaining strawberries and chill or freeze it until ready to serve.

Raw food is in! Raw desserts are an easy place to start, since so many of the components of a happening dessert are often served raw. I'm certainly going to experiment in this area and you might want to also.

If you can't eat nuts, you could use extra dates and other dried fruits put through a food processor till they turn to a paste. Try adding some oats, bran flakes, etc. That'll bind your crust together.

Nutty Strawberry Pie

Rich Tofu Mousse

The tofu acts as a dairy replacement here, but it's the bananas and other things that give the terrific flavor. This is wonderful deeply chilled as the refreshing finish to a meal.

1 package silken tofu, chilled
3 frozen bananas
soy milk for blending if necessary
2 Tbsp (30 mL) carob powder or
    vegan cocoa powder
2 Tbsp (30 mL) maple syrup or honey†
fresh or thawed, frozen berries to top with if desired
fresh mint leaves to top if available

Peel the frozen bananas and cut into small pieces, for blending.

Combine the ingredients (except the berries) by blending them with an upright or hand blender—you'll need to add some soy milk to the frozen bananas. Or use a food processor and then the soy milk won't be needed. If possible, chill for 15 minutes or so, to set before serving. Spoon the mixture into individual parfait dishes or champagne flutes. Then top with the berries and a mint leaf and serve.

† VEGAN OPTION agave syrup, brown rice syrup or barley malt syrup

To freeze bananas, you can just throw them in the freezer in their peels. When they're ready to use (fully frozen), just carefully remove the peels with a sharp knife. You can thaw them for 5–10 minutes, or quickly run them under hot water before peeling if they're rock-solid.

Quick Trip to the Tropics: Instead of the carob powder and berries, you could use some fine coconut and a bit of tropical fruit.

Here's something that works brilliantly with or without the carob—pistachios! Use enough finely crushed ones to replace the carob if you want a beautiful banana pistachio mousse, or just add some pistachios to this dessert for a gorgeous addition.

Perfect Almond-Berry Pie

Any time you have quality ingredients, and you don't cook them, all the better. More of the nutrients will be intact and the taste difference is so worthwhile.

3 cups (750 mL) dates, chopped
    as finely as you can

4 cups (1 L) almonds, crushed or
    finely chopped

2 cups (500 mL) pecans, crushed or finely chopped

olive oil for the pan

4 cups berries (fresh or frozen, thawed)

3 cups (750 mL) soy milk

1 cup (250 mL) sugar

pinch of cinnamon

good pinch of salt

2 tsp (10 mL) vanilla

2 cups (500 mL) soy yogurt

a few berries and almonds for garnishing

Simply combine the dates, almonds and pecans and mash with a fork into a ball. (Heh heh—it sounds so easy but it takes a bit of mashing. If you have a food processor, you might want to employ that baby!) Press into a 10-inch (25-cm) olive-oiled pie pan, or a small lasagna pan, as flat as you can get it.

Then add the fruit layer into the bottom of the crust—gorgeous! Next, take the remaining ingredients, except the yogurt, and whiz them all up with a hand blender until thick, adding more almonds if necessary. It should be a thick, pudding-like consistency. Then, mix in the yogurt and spread it over the top. Chill until you're ready to serve. Decorate the top with a few berries and/or almonds if desired.

Fruit and nuts are an ancient, amazing combination. They work perfectly in this gorgeous pie. If you want some other great combos, try peach and pecan, mango and macadamia nut, or cherry and almond—delicious.

This pie has even more charm if you do little tartlets—just make them in muffin tins for a perfect size.

You could also use a terrine pan, line it with plastic wrap, and then press in the crust mixture. Then add a berry layer, another crust layer, and a berry layer, gently pressing down each layer. Chill. Pull out the plastic wrap to gently unmold. Cut into pieces and serve.

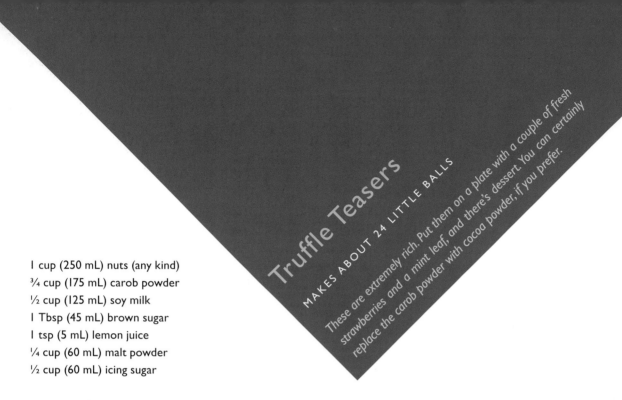

Truffle Teasers

MAKES ABOUT 24 LITTLE BALLS

These are extremely rich. Put them on a plate with a couple of fresh strawberries and a mint leaf, and there's dessert. You can certainly replace the carob powder with cocoa powder, if you prefer.

1 cup (250 mL) nuts (any kind)
¾ cup (175 mL) carob powder
½ cup (125 mL) soy milk
1 Tbsp (45 mL) brown sugar
1 tsp (5 mL) lemon juice
¼ cup (60 mL) malt powder
½ cup (60 mL) icing sugar

Put ½ cup (125 mL) of the nuts, ¼ cup (60 mL) carob powder, all of the soy milk, the brown sugar and the lemon juice into a deep container. Whiz it up with a hand blender or in a food processor. Set aside.

Put the remaining ½ cup (125 mL) of carob powder in a bowl and press it with a spoon to remove any lumps. Chop or crush the remainder of the nuts, add them to the carob powder and mix in the malt powder. Then slowly add the wet mixture to the carob mixture and combine well, ensuring to press out any lumps in the carob. Stir in the malt powder. Cover and refrigerate for an hour, or put it in the freezer for about 15 minutes, or until cold enough to manipulate.

On a parchment covered plate, sprinkle ¼ cup (60 mL) of icing sugar. Make little 1-inch balls with a teaspoon. Then sprinkle the rest of the icing sugar over the top. Roll each little ball in the icing sugar until round and well covered. They melt quickly, so store them in the fridge or freezer (they're yummy frozen). I would say these are better cold than at room temperature; they tend to melt.

If you want a truffle that won't melt, you can always add ingredients with body (crushed or powdered nuts, wheat germ, oat bran, etc.) to the base, before adding the icing sugar. However, this is supposed to be heavy on the carob/chocolate: cloying, decadent. So, try them as is, even though they're more of a hassle to roll this way.

If you like coconut, you can roll them in that instead of the powdered sugar. Little carob or cocoa macaroons!

Try rolling them in crushed nuts or a bit of cinnamon, or an icing sugar/cinnamon mix. If you're giving them as a gift, it's always cool to have ONE that has a different coating—the coveted one in the box!

Wanna be trendy? Chocolate and salt is in. Put a few truffles on a tray (whether sugared or not) and sprinkle lightly with coarse sea salt. Fleur de Sel is an expensive French one if you're into that.

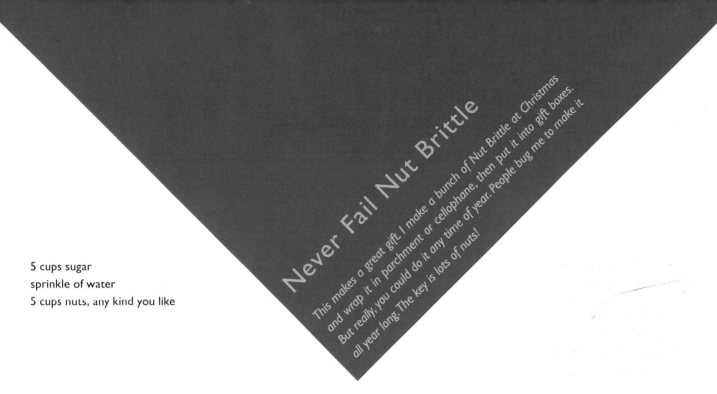

Never Fail Nut Brittle

This makes a great gift. I make a bunch of Nut Brittle at Christmas and wrap it in parchment or cellophane, then put it into gift boxes. But really, you could do it any time of year. People bug me to make it all year long. The key is lots of nuts!

5 cups sugar
sprinkle of water
5 cups nuts, any kind you like

Put the sugar into a dry pan over medium-low heat. Sprinkle the sugar with ¼ cup (60 mL) or so of water, stirring constantly. When the sugar becomes liquidy and begins turning a caramel color, turn the heat down to low and continue. When it's all liquid and light golden brown, add the nuts immediately. Mix well. Turn the mixture out onto a large surface covered in parchment paper. Do this VERY CAREFULLY (it's shockingly hot). Spread it out quickly with a metal spatula. It hardens up fast. Wait until it's dry and not too hot to touch. It only takes a few minutes. Break it up into chunks for a very festive and natural candy.

Be careful! You could break a tooth on this stuff, so use caution and only bite into the ultra-nutty parts. I'd recommend that kids only suck the small pieces.

What I love about making this is that to make most candy requires a candy thermometer and you don't need one here, as long as you don't burn it. Just keep your heat low, and watch it and stir it constantly.

You can crush this up finely to sprinkle over ice cream, or to use anywhere you might put sprinkles, like on top of a cupcake.

When pouring out your brittle, you could do it in small lollipop-sized circles. Then add a popsicle stick while wet and you have gourmet lollipops. These are also great for gifts.

The clean-up for this isn't as scary as it first appears. Your hard-as-a-rock, caramel-covered pan can be soaked for 20 minutes or so in hot water (to dissolve the sugars) and it will be a breeze to clean.

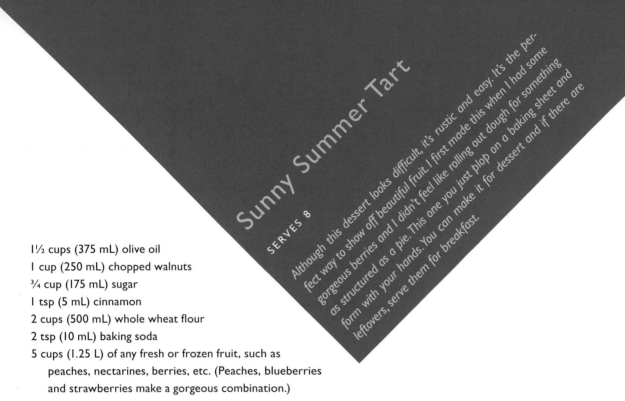

Sunny Summer Tart

SERVES 8

Although this dessert looks difficult, it's rustic and easy. It's the perfect way to show off beautiful fruit. I first made this when I had some gorgeous berries and I didn't feel like rolling out dough for something as structured as a pie. This one you just plop on a baking sheet and form with your hands. You can make it for dessert and if there are leftovers, serve them for breakfast.

1½ cups (375 mL) olive oil

1 cup (250 mL) chopped walnuts

¾ cup (175 mL) sugar

1 tsp (5 mL) cinnamon

2 cups (500 mL) whole wheat flour

2 tsp (10 mL) baking soda

5 cups (1.25 L) of any fresh or frozen fruit, such as peaches, nectarines, berries, etc. (Peaches, blueberries and strawberries make a gorgeous combination.)

Preheat oven to 425°F (220°C).

Combine olive oil, walnuts, ¼ cup of the sugar, cinnamon, flour and baking soda in a bowl. Mix well. Slowly add about 1 cup (250 mL) water until it forms a slightly wetter than usual pie-type dough. It doesn't have to be exact.

If you have parchment, line a 9-inch (1.5-L) pie plate or baking sheet with that, otherwise lightly grease the pan. Flour your hands and simply press the dough into the pan or sheet to about ½ inch (1 cm) thick. If it's thicker, that's just fine.

Put the fruit on top and turn the edges in slightly around the fruit to form a tart. Sprinkle the remainder of the sugar on top. You could add additional cinnamon if desired.

Bake the tart for about 25 minutes or until the tart edge is golden brown and firm to the touch. Remove the tart from the oven and let it cool for half an hour if possible so that the fruit will set and the crust will absorb the liquid.

You can serve the tart slices with some soy yogurt or a non-dairy vanilla ice cream if desired. The yogurt is especially nice for breakfast, with the tart reheated.

Another stunning tart combination is to use lots of thinly sliced apples and season them with cinnamon, powdered ginger, a squirt of citrus juice and brown sugar. After baking, dot with a few fresh blackberries.

Dusting a tart with a light sprinkling of powdered sugar, cinnamon or carob powder is a great way to finish it. Lightly shake a fine strainer with the powder of your choice over the tart, for the finest coating possible. Finish it with a mint leaf in the middle.

Pineapple Pine Nut Parfait

SERVES 4

This is an old Italian dessert, but the original contained butter. I've added the cinnamon stick here, but I'm fairly sure I've seen other additions over the years. If you don't want cinnamon, just leave it out, or add a few fresh mint leaves—that'd be great too.

1 Tbsp (15 mL) olive oil
½ cinnamon stick
2 cups (500 mL) pineapple chunks
1 cup (250 mL) pine nuts
sprinkle of cinnamon or fresh mint leaves,
    to garnish

Put the olive oil and cinnamon stick into a pan. Heat it up to medium-high and then add the pineapple. You won't believe the aroma! Stir constantly and cook for a minute or two, before adding the pine nuts. When the pineapple edges begin to brown lightly, remove it from the heat.

Serve this as is, in parfait dishes or in martini glasses, for a beautiful, simple dessert.

Or, serve it topped with a vegan vanilla ice cream, or topped with pine nut cream, below.

PINE NUT CREAM
1 cup (250 mL) pine nuts
soy milk to blend
1 tsp (5 mL) vanilla
1 tsp (5 mL) maple syrup

For the Pine Nut Cream: blend all the ingredients in a food processor, or with an upright or hand blender. If you're using a blender you'll need the soy milk. If you do it in the food processor, just add 1 Tbsp (15 mL) or so of soy milk to flavor it. Blend it until it's smooth and thick.

Put a dollop of the pine nut cream on top of each parfait. Decorate each with a mint leaf or a sprinkle of cinnamon.

To make this even more sublime, serve it with a rich espresso coffee in its full, non-milky glory. A perfect contrast!

This dessert is just as good cool or at room temperature as right out of the pan. So it's perfect for taking on romantic picnics!

Have you ever barbecued pineapple? Just stick a skewer through it and pop it on the barbie. Some people dip it in chocolate after it's cooked, but the hot pineapple is great just plain.

You could put one teeny drop of peppermint extract into the pine nut cream if you're making it. That makes it even fresher, a cool note against the cloyingly sweet and tangy hot pineapple.

When I was a kid, I could have spent all day in my grandmother's pantry. It was full of things to explore and smelled great. She sure wasn't a vegan—and now that I think of it, she didn't keep a ton of food in there. She kept dry goods, olive oil and vinegar, spices and pots and pans in her pantry. Mostly though, I remember a lot of board games and a glass squirt bottle of Jergens hand cream that I would kill to have now, for nostalgia's sake.

Vegan and vegetarian ingredients used to be difficult to find. Today, because healthier eating and lifestyles are on the rise, more and more of these products can be found in a regular supermarket. Whole grains are appearing on the menus of upscale restaurants, most supermarkets have introduced organics sections and some markets specialize in organic foods. Now, V Cuisine is an accessible, manageable lifestyle possibility.

The best reason to keep a pantry well-stocked, is to take the trauma out of meal preparation when you're in a rush. Also, you won't be tempted to get fast food when you can whip up something better in half an hour.

To make your pantry fantastic, fun and inspiring, keep some items on hand that you know make life easier. A variety of grains, beans and some canned goods will start you off. Add spices and herbs that get you jazzed about cooking and a few exotic ingredients, and you're on your way. A few games won't hurt either—or whatever indulgence you want to squirrel away in there.

Here are a few things I like to keep in my pantry.

Grains

BARLEY (HULLED BARLEY OR BARLEY GROATS) This is the least processed form of barley; only the inedible outer hull is removed. It takes longer to cook than pot barley and pearl barley, but it makes a marvelous addition to soups or a great side dish.

BUCKWHEAT (GROATS/RAW, UNTOASTED) These have the outer hull (inedible) removed and then they're crushed to a smaller consistency. Some people think they're bitter, so they only eat them toasted or roasted (kasha). You can use buckwheat in cereals and baking, or in place of rice.

BULGAR WHEAT This is whole wheat that has been soaked and baked to make it easier to cook. I like to have some of the coarser grainy one on hand for making Taboulleh or a variety of quick salads. It's great because it doesn't have to be cooked—just reconstitute it with water.

KAMUT Kamut is actually a brand name, but through common usage, this type of wheat is now referred to as kamut. Use it as you would any wheat berry; it has a particularly nice flavor.

QUINOA I love to keep some of this around to make quick and delicious meals. It's an ancient grain that you can practically live off of with its well-balanced protein content (the Incas did). It's fluffy, it's yummy—the perfect bed for vegetarian delights.

RYE (BERRIES, WHOLE GRAIN) These possess the lovely and distinct flavor of rye in its natural form. They have great taste and texture.

SPELT This is another ancient grain that's popular now. It contains gluten, but is more easily tolerated for some people who are allergic to wheat. It's deliciously chewy and rich with nutrients.

TRITICALE This is a wheat/rye hybrid with a hint of both flavors. It's easier to grow in soil of poorer quality than most whole grains. It's super-high in protein.

WHEAT (BERRIES, WHOLE GRAIN) These nutty-tasting wheat grains have a great, somewhat chewy texture.

WHEAT (CRACKED) This is whole wheat that's been cut into tiny pieces for quick cooking. It makes a nice hot breakfast cereal.

WHEAT GERM Within the kernel of the whole grain is the embryo, which is usually referred to as the germ. Although wheat germ is ultra-nutritious, it doesn't have a long shelf-life, so refrigerate it if you aren't going to use it right away. I add it to breads, cookies, muffins and the like for added richness. Sometimes I add it to smoothies, just for a boost.

Rice

There are other varieties of rice that you can make risotto with, they're just harder to find. If you frequent Italian markets though, ask, and you're sure to find them. Arborio also comes in a brown version (yay! more fiber and nutrients), but it isn't as creamy as the white.

BASMATI RICE   The scent of this stuff is like nothing else. It's found in the Himalayas and it's the ultimate accompaniment to Indian food. I always keep some on hand. It's a long-grain rice and it also comes in a brown variety.

BROWN RICE   This is a staple food in my household. It doesn't matter if it's short or long grain (I buy both). I use it as a side dish or as the base for a main course. The brown rice retains more nutrients—including the bran and germ.

STICKY RICE (SUSHI RICE, GLUTINOUS RICE)   This ultra-sticky rice makes the perfect ingredient for sushi and goes alongside anything Japanese-inspired. I love to make California rolls, cucumber maki and other vegan delights, so I try to always have some of this around.

WILD RICE   I'm obsessed with the stuff. It's not even rice—it's a grass seed. I love the exotic look of it and the textural bite it provides. Since it's expensive, most people only mix it into a pilaf, which is great.

How to Cook Rice

I recently used a rice cooker for the first time. Most appliances aren't that impressive, but this thing is a miracle. If you have one, just use that!

Every variety of rice has a different character and different cooking times, but when cooking regular white rice the rule of thumb is two parts water to one part rice. I use a bit more for brown rice, perhaps 2½ or 3 to 1.

Bring the water to a boil in a pot with a tight-fitting lid. Add the rice, and immediately turn the heat down to the lowest possible heat that'll maintain a simmer. As soon as the water is mostly cooked away, turn the heat to "barely there," always keeping it covered. If that's more than say, 15 minutes, turn off the heat.

There will be detailed instructions for each specific type of rice and grain on my website at www.vcuisine.com.

Cans & Jars

ARTICHOKES   I always keep a couple of cans of plain artichokes and a big jar of the marinated ones. As usual, read those labels—sometimes they put a lot of junky oils into these things. They are great to have on hand for making dips or serving with crackers and some olives: instant antipasto!

BEANS   Although I buy navy beans, kidney beans, black beans, chickpeas (and all the rest) dried, I also keep a big supply of canned ones. I just don't always have time to reconstitute the dried ones.

FRUIT   I like to have a few special canned organic fruits as treats. Sometimes these are baby pineapple rings, lychee nuts or an organic pie filling. These are for those times when you have no time to make something. It happens!

NUTS   Since they can go bad, I only like to keep large quantities of nuts that I use often. Even when they don't spoil, they lose their flavor, like spices when not used in a timely fashion. The ones I use constantly are shelled pecans, almonds, walnuts and cashews. I also like to keep a bag of the ones with shells.

NUT BUTTERS You can get any kind of nut butter. I love cashew and almond butters. I like to keep an organic jar of each from the natural food store. They're beautiful in baking or for rich desserts, like for binding a raw pie crust together. Try sunflower seed butter, which is delicious in dips.

OLIVES I like to keep a selection on hand: kalamatas, some big green ones, the canned black olives for pizzas and such. I usually have some jarred and canned, and some in the fridge as well.

ROASTED RED PEPPERS It's another must-have specialty item. Roast them yourself or find them in jars in most supermarkets.

Mustards

Just as there are zillions of vinegars, the same is true of mustards. I think I love 'em all! There's a kind of sweet hot mustard I like so much I could eat the damn thing as a dip. The heat of hot mustards ranges from super mild to near death. You can get mustards made with every kind of wine or herb on the planet. Try 'em all if you can afford to do so. Or make your own. I rarely use mustard as a condiment—I consider it a potential ingredient for every savory recipe.

Oils

OLIVE OIL When you choose an olive oil, pick one that's cold-pressed. It means that no heat was involved in the processing so the vitamins remain intact. For dishes that aren't cooked, use extra virgin (the first pressing of the olives, with all the good stuff in it). If you use a lot of olive oil, as I do, go for organic if at all possible. I only use extra virgin olive oil—I find it's the same price because I buy it in such a large container.

OTHER OIL I use flaxseed oil on salads and things because I like the flavor and flax has great health benefits—it's high in nutrients and good for your skin. You can find sesame and flaxseed oils in the refrigerated section of a natural foods store.

Vinegars

Vinegar is great for adding depth of flavor, in addition to the zing it provides. Its acidity balances oils, so feel free to use it in cooking as well as salad dressings. There are so many great vinegars out there. The following are what I consider staples for my pantry.

APPLE CIDER VINEGAR This is a nice tangy vinegar that adds a particular taste and brings out the greatness in certain raw vegetables and cooked potatoes. I use this or lemon in most potato salads. In the past few years it's gotten a lot of press about its health benefits.

BALSAMIC VINEGAR The real thing is only from Modena, Italy. It's taken super seriously, with a big checklist of quality controls just like with fine wines. It ranges from reasonably priced to deadly expensive. It's a must for adding richness, color, depth and sweetness to recipes.

MALT VINEGAR This one has a deep flavor that's a nice switch from the others it's all about keeping your palate awake! I switch this for apple cider vinegar sometimes when I feel like it. It also makes a great addition to barbecue sauces.

RED WINE VINEGAR This is great for all salads, I use this as an everyday vinegar. I never buy the white stuff except to clean my coffee pot.

RICE VINEGAR   This one is great for all things Asian, and when you want to keep it light. It's the vinegar that flavors sushi rice. It's lovely on any raw veggies, especially things like matchstick carrots and simple salads.

OTHER VINEGAR   On occasion I buy raspberry vinegar, white wine vinegar, herb-infused vinegars, etc. There are champagne vinegars. There's umeboshi vinegar, made from umeboshi plums, with a distinct Japanese flavor that works well in certain dishes. You can get vinegars infused with so many things; check out the ones that interest you.

Sauces

HOISIN SAUCE   This is another great sauce that can be used in endless ways. It's quite sweet. My favorite use for it is to stir-fry extra firm tofu strips and a lot of vegetables, pour on the Hoisin and make lettuce wraps. Use extra crispy iceberg lettuce. To die for!

LOUISIANA HOT SAUCE   I like to keep a good bottle of this around (hot, but thinned with vinegar, so not too harsh). It's good for revving up a dish that needs a little something.

MIRIN   This rice wine is low on alcohol and has a distinctive taste. It's sometimes used for flavoring sushi rice and works in all things Japanese, or with light springy vegetables.

MISO   This Japanese invention is a paste made of a fermented grain (usually soybeans, but also rice, barley, etc.) combined with salt, soy sauce and other ingredients such as wine. It makes a fabulous soup base, is an excellent flavoring for salad dressings, stews, gravies, cooked veggies and grains. It's a staple in my pantry. Some varieties are dark, others light. Experiment, because the character of the various misos can be quite varied.

PLUM SAUCE   I like to keep a good pre-made one on hand for making spring rolls. These are the kind of items that help you to give up takeout.

SOY SAUCE   This is a major flavor in my kitchen and I don't reserve it for Asian foods. I use it constantly—it works perfectly with grains and veggies, especially leafy greens. I always keep a good, name brand soy sauce (Japanese, sushi quality) in my pantry. I also keep a good bottle of teriyaki sauce (the thin kind) and a bottle of some kind of tempura dipping sauce. They're great flavor builders.

SRIRACHA   Some people call this rooster sauce because one brand has a rooster on the bottle. It's sublime. It's hot, but the flavor is incredible so a little works wonders. You can take a bowl of ordinary baked beans and make it insanely good with this terrific concoction.

TABASCO SAUCE   A few drops of this can really up the taste factor in anything. It also comes in a green version so you can dot some red and green embellishments on fancy little party foods.

Spices

CAROB POWDER   This comes from a pod and my kids love the stuff. I often use it in baking. In any recipe that requires carob powder, you can successfully replace it with a good-quality cocoa powder if you like. Carob has a third of the calories of cocoa. People who have allergies to chocolate can often tolerate carob.

JAMAICA ME CRAZY   This is the only name-brand spice blend I use regularly. I buy the seasoned sea salt and the seasoned pepper. This stuff is great on lots of things, especially anything grilled. You will fly straight to heaven if you use it on grilled mushrooms.

NUTRITIONAL YEAST   This is a good source of protein and B complex vitamins and it's pretty delicious. Some brands have Vitamin B_{12} added. It's great for flavoring popcorn, sauces, and sprinkling on pasta and pizza.

Snacks

I always try to keep a supply of decent, whole grain pretzels around. True, they're a sort of junk food, but there are worse things, as we all know. Just read the labels and always get the best ones. I also keep a box or two of good crackers and a bag of tortilla chips.

Other Asian Delights

I like to keep some wasabi (hot Japanese horseradish) around for sushi, or adding to salad dressings, vegetables, etc. It comes powdered in little cans and is easy to reconstitute with water or it comes in tubes, ready to use.

Another must is nori, the dark seaweed (often toasted) that you wrap around sushi. Kids are quite happy to munch on the stuff plain, bizarre as that might be. It's great for them—loaded with vitamins and minerals, so it makes a great quick snack.

There are lots of other forms of seaweed that come packaged in your natural foods store or Asian section of the supermarket. Some are great for adding to soups, stews and other dishes. Try some anytime—they add some serious nutrition.

ASAFETIDA (OR ASAFOETIDA)   This is a weird and wonderful flavoring that I adore, perhaps because it's found often in Indian food. It's sometimes referred to as "fetid" or "foul-smelling" but I think that's in reference to the plant. The powdered stuff is pungent, but kind of garlic or onion-like. I like to throw some in exotic sauces, such as curries.

Index